## THANK YOU

To Dr Stephanie May, Dr Mark Bellingham, Dr Peter Bellingham, Dr Mick Clout, and Mita Harris for generously sharing their time, enthusiasm and extensive knowledge of kererū; and for casting their expert eyes over the contents. Thanks also to Rod MacKinnon for tweaking the beat of the verse and Jenny Bennett for the soft background image of nikau. Any errors or omissions are entirely my own.

First published in 2018 by Reed New Holland Publishers
London • Sydney • Auckland

131–151 Great Titchfield Street, London W1W 5BB, United Kingdom
1/66 Gibbes Street, Chatswood, NSW 2067, Australia
5/39 Woodside Ave, Northcote, Auckland 0627, New Zealand

newhollandpublishers.com

Copyright © 2018 Reed New Holland Publishers
Copyright © 2018 in text and images: Terry Fitzgibbon

All rights reserved. No part of this publication may be reproduced, stored in a retrieval system or transmitted, in any form or by any means, electronic, mechanical, photocopying, recording or otherwise, without the prior written permission of the publishers and copyright holders.

A catalogue record for this book is available from the National Library of New Zealand.

ISBN 9781869665173

Group Managing Director: Fiona Schultz
Publisher: Sarah Beresford
Project Editor: Rebecca Sutherland
Production Director: James Mills-Hicks
Printed in China by Easy Fame (Hong Kong) Limited

10 9 8 7 6 5 4 3 2 1

Keep up with New Holland Publishers on Facebook
facebook.com/NewHollandPublishers

# Coo-Coo KERERŪ

Terry Fitzgibbon

Kererū helped Māui haul
the North Island from wild seas.
Now mokopuna* of this bird
spread big seeds of native trees.

✳ = descendants

When someone says **"pigeons"** most people think of **little bobbing birds** that roost on tall buildings, peck around city parks, or poop on statues.

But New Zealand is also home to **big beautiful pigeons** — kererū.
These native birds live in and around our forests, farms and settlements.

Whooshing winged glider
in a glossy blue-green suit.

... Will even hang upside-down to gobble forest fruit.

Kererū surely deserve the nickname "greedy-guts".
Do they **look smart**? **Yes!**
**Brain smart**? Well maybe **not always** . . .

Has a bob-bob-bobbing head
and a scarlet bullet beak.
Wears a bright, white singlet
and fluffy pants over red feet.

Kererū often bob their heads up-down-n'-around. This is **smart** as it helps them stay in tune with their surroundings, including watching out for hunting falcons while eating.

Kererū's big fruit lunches
make their bellies choc-a-block tight.
After this fruit-stew brews in the sun
they may tumble in bumbling flight.

After guzzling a heavy load of fruit, kererū often bungle their take-off and crash down through the undergrowth or even into car or house windows. A Northland bird-rescue centre claims that if kererū scoff a tummy-full of tropical fruit such as guavas, then roost in the warm sun, the fruit-mix turns into a boozy brew. They suggest this causes kererū to become quite tipsy – so their next flight is risky – especially if they topple to the ground. **Not** a **smart** place to be if stray cats are lurking!

All this pooping helps spread native trees around kererū's forest homes and elsewhere too. Of course, when these seeds grow into trees they enrich nature and also become food sources for kererū's *mokopuna.**

**mokopuna* = descendants

Claps, flaps and flutters wings
to spark-up a new romance.
Flirts with fanned tail feathers
in a cooing, wooing dance.

Kererū courtships are long-lasting and quite comical. The male shows off to the female by fluttering upwards and clapping his wings before gliding back with tail spread downwards. If he is lucky, this might lead to cooing and feather-preening sessions. If this is followed by 'billing' (when the female puts her beak inside the male's beak), the romance is progressing well.

The pair choose a forked branch and weave a cradle of sticks. Although this nest looks messy, it shelters newborn chicks.

The female kererū lays a single egg in their shallow nest of tangled twigs. This is generally high, well hidden and shaded from the sun. The male and female take turns to keep the egg warm for a month before it hatches.

Sly and sneaky possums
come skulking into nests,
to chomp a chick or slurp an egg.
Let's wipe out these pesky pests!

Predators such as stoats, wild cats, possums and ship rats are the most serious threat to the kererū. They eat their eggs and young. Stoats and cats will also attack and kill adult kererū.

Each fluffy kererū chick is fed a rich milky brew. Then gradually the parents add lumpy chunks of seedy stew.

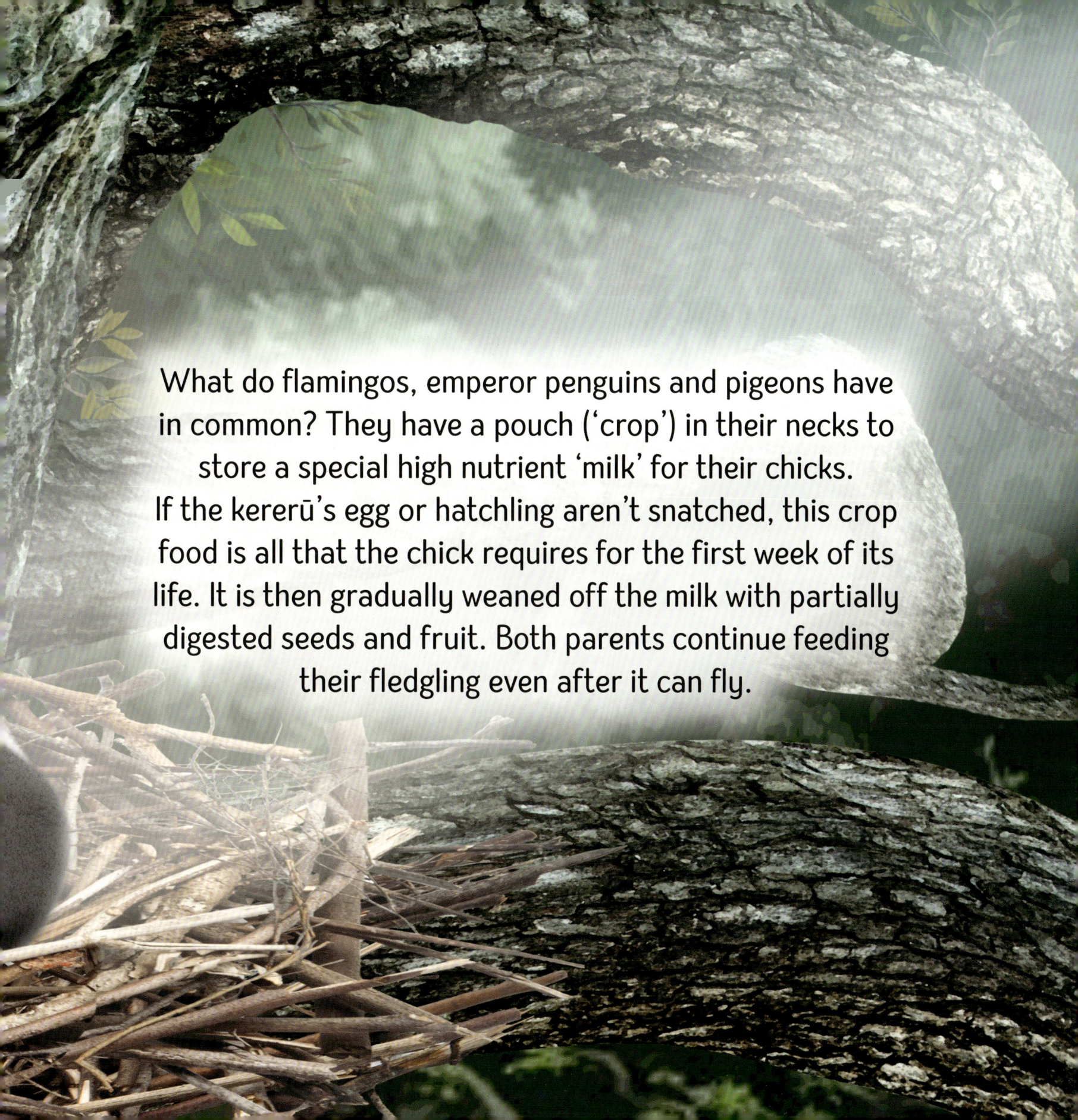

What do flamingos, emperor penguins and pigeons have in common? They have a pouch ('crop') in their necks to store a special high nutrient 'milk' for their chicks.
If the kererū's egg or hatchling aren't snatched, this crop food is all that the chick requires for the first week of its life. It is then gradually weaned off the milk with partially digested seeds and fruit. Both parents continue feeding their fledgling even after it can fly.

When winter's cold cloak creeps in
with snow and chilly showers,
some sip the drips of icicles
or crunch on frosted flowers.

Kererū drink using their beaks like straws to suck up water. Most birds scoop water and then tilt their head back to swallow.
In late winter kererū often feed on kōwhai and tree lucerne. They sometimes get so carried away they rip the flowers and leaves to shreds. Thankfully these hardy trees will bounce back from this very rough trimming.

Blustery wind glider
zooming updraft rider,
whirling ... swirling,
swooping ... looping,
twirling to 'n' fro.
A flashy shuffle
a flirty hustle ...
A sky-high tango show!

Kererū are wizards at swooping and soaring on valley updrafts. Keep a look-out for one of their most spectacular displays during their breeding season. The male bird gains height with noisy wing-beats, stalls with its body vertical, wings and tail spread, then tilts forwards — or sometimes sideways — to glide gracefully down again.
Amazing eye-catching performances!

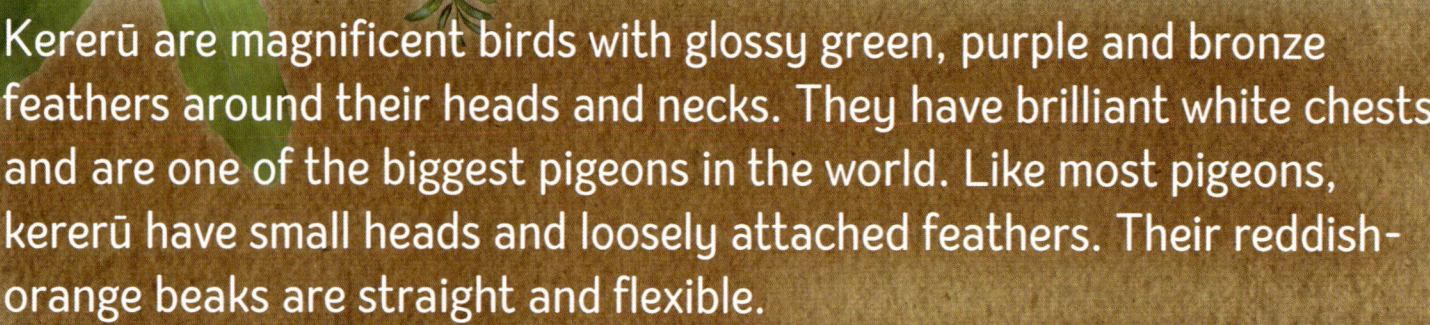

Kererū are magnificent birds with glossy green, purple and bronze feathers around their heads and necks. They have brilliant white chests and are one of the biggest pigeons in the world. Like most pigeons, kererū have small heads and loosely attached feathers. Their reddish-orange beaks are straight and flexible.

Kererū can weigh between 550–850 grams when fully grown and can measure up to 51cm from tail to beak.

Kererū have lots of different names. Some people call them wood pigeons although they are a jumbo version of the Pacific wood ('fruit') pigeons. Their Māori name is kererū, although some iwi in Northland call them kūkupa, and kūkū. On the Chatham Islands kererū have 'cousins' called *parea*. They are similar looking but larger, and not as brightly coloured. Their scientific name is *Hemiphaga novaeseelandiae.*

Kererū's home is mainly low to mid-altitude forests from Northland to Stewart Island. They will visit and live in towns or cities especially where large fruit trees are growing. Kererū are very capable fliers. They will search for food trees in their home territories which can extend to over 30,000 ha. Kererū's whumping wing-beat is one of the most distinctive sounds in our forests.

### Long distance seed-spreaders

Because moa and other big-seed eaters are extinct, kererū are now the only long-distance seed-spreaders of large forest fruit such as taraire, pūriri, karaka and tawāpou. Their beak width ('gape') allows them to swallow berries up to 25mm. They also spread the fruit of around 70 other native plants including their favourite miro berries. Kererū will also eat willows, broom and even clover.

Farmland expansion over the years has seen many native forests split into small pockets. These remnants need seeds from elsewhere to flourish and survive. Hooray for the long-distance-flying kererū! In a single day a kererū can fly 70km. They have even been recorded crossing both Foveaux and Cook Straits. Their ancestors from Norfolk Island and the Kermadecs must have flown even further.

## Warm climate 'hatchers'

When there is plenty of fruit available in northern Aotearoa, kererū can hatch more than one chick per year over the breeding season. Further south, where fewer large fruiting trees grow, they generally only raise one chick between October and April.

Chicks leave the nest when they are 30 to 55 days old, but the parents continue feeding them for up to four weeks. Their 'kererū kindy' bonding can continue for a further two years. This allows the young to learn where and when to fly to fresh food sources.

## History and threats

Pigeons were around Aotearoa long before humans landed on our shores. Sixteen million year old fossils from a now extinct pigeon were recently unearthed in Central Otago.

Birdland Aotearoa has been severely trashed since humans arrived here. Before Māori landed on our shores, forests covered 85 percent of the entire country. Now this has been reduced to 23 percent. Less forest means less food for kererū, and fewer places for them to nest and live. Although large forest areas were burnt earlier by Māori while hunting, most forest destruction occurred after the arrival of Europeans.

In those earlier times Māori hunted kererū routinely. They ate kererū fresh, or cooked and preserved them in gourds or in totara bark (*patūa*) as food reserves (*huahua*). However, early records suggest that Māori cultural protection measures (*rāhui*) allowed kererū numbers to sometimes recover. Unfortunately the huge flocks of kererū the early settlers witnessed no longer exist today. Native forest clearances for farmland and forestry, plus overkill by both Māori and Pākehā hunters obviously took a huge toll on kererū's habitat and numbers.

Along with over 70 exotic birds, the European settlers also introduced a massive number of mammals including predators such as cats, rats, stoats and possums. Predators are really bad news for kererū. Possums are the major culprits as they rob their nests of eggs and chicks, compete for the same food, and stop tree growth by munching new shoots.

Kererū's life expectancy has dropped from 20–25 years to just 5–6 years. This drop is largely due to loss of their forest homes, introduced predators and food competitors, collisions with cars and windows, plus illegal poaching – although kererū are now fully protected under law.

Most New Zealanders want these birds to thrive. Recent records show that our communities appreciate their reappearance in towns and cities. We all need to work together to increase kererū numbers.

**Here are 7 helpful ideas:**

1. If you go looking for kererū, don't bash through the bush. Move as silently as possible. When you spot one, just sit down and quietly watch — you will get to experience what an awesome bird they are.
2. Place decorations or a window protector on windows that are likely to be hit by them. If a kererū flies into your window wait to see if it will recover. Just keep your pets away.
3. Plant kererū food sources in your garden, especially pūriri, tawa, kōwhai, hīnau, hohere, and tree lucerne.
4. Encourage the adults you live with to set up a trap to catch possums, rats and stoats in your garden, around your family farm or community. The kererū will come back to a pest-free environment.
5. Comply with "Slow Down for Kererū" signs. Wellington City has erected these on busy roadsides near bush reserves.
6. If you find a sick or injured kererū, take it to your nearest bird-rescue centre as soon as possible or call the Department of Conservation on 0800 DOCHOT.
7. To catch an injured kererū, throw a towel or net over it, scoop it up (gently holding its wings to its sides so they don't get damaged) and put it in a box padded with soft cloth and some ventilation holes.
8. Join a Kiwi Conservation Club or Forest & Bird branch.

## Final words . . .

New Zealand's native wildlife has experienced many boom and bust cycles since early human settlement. Hopefully the worst years of bust for birds are over and the boom years are well and truly on the way.

Birds are one of the last remaining branches on the dinosaur tree — they matter, our kererū especially so. Nobody in their right mind would want to see this amazing bird go the way of the moa!

## Key online resources

https://kererudiscovery.org.nz/about-kereru
http://www.backyardbirds.co.nz/bird_feeding6.htm
http://www.projectkereru.org.nz

## The author/illustrator

TERRY FITZGIBBON is an enthusiast for protecting Aotearoa's wild native species. Protecting forests is the theme of his University thesis. Terry has worked for both Forest & Bird and the Department of Conservation.

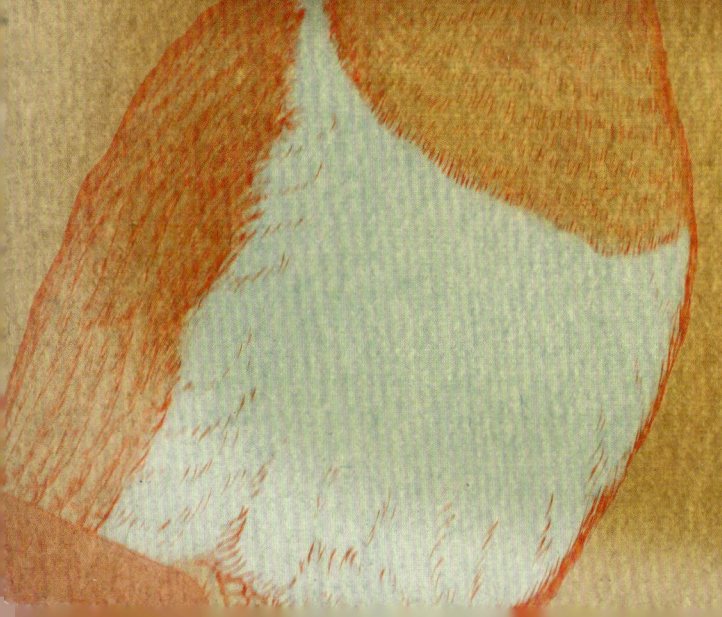

# MICHEL ROUX

*Best wishes, Michel*

## sauces for fish & shellfish

**Dedication**
To my son Alain, who cooks side-by-side with me at The Waterside Inn.

# Contents

| | |
|---|---|
| 4 | Foreword |
| 7 | **About Sauces** |
| 8 | Practical Advice |
| 10 | Stocks |
| 14 | Roux |
| 15 | Mayonnaise |
| 17 | **Recipes** |
| 18 | 'Instant' Sauces |
| 20 | Vegetable Coulis |
| 22 | Flavoured Butters and Oil |
| 28 | Sauces for Fish and Shellfish |
| 63 | Index |

# Foreword

The key to preparing a successful sauce for fish and shellfish is to follow a few very simple rules. Fish and shellfish are delicate creatures, which inspire the creation of light sauces, rather modern in style, such as nages, beurre blanc, vegetable coulis and sabayons, as well as flavoured butters which melt gently over the flesh of poached or grilled fish.

You can use spirits, wine, fresh herbs and spices in these sauces, but they must be used judiciously and parsimoniously so as not to mask the fine, delicate flavour and texture of the fish and shellfish. On the contrary, they should bring a harmony and subtlety to the seafood. It is vitally important to use only the freshest herbs and spices to ensure that you create a perfectly balanced sauce.

My mother always used to say that the foods which come from the sea are among the tastiest, most tender and most natural. Fruits of the sea need only a very little sauce to enhance them without swamping them; any sauces for seafood need careful thought to achieve the perfect balance. When Maman prepared moules marinières, the aroma would waft out of the casserole, filling the air with the iodised scents of the sea. She only used shallots in this dish, never garlic, whose flavour she considered too aggressive for the delicate flesh of the little bouchot mussels.

On high days and holy days, the succulent mayonnaise she served with a cold poached codling was a treat for the palate. She could never understand why anyone needed to buy ready-made bottled mayonnaise. Holding her bowl with one hand and a fork in the other, she would rotate the fork in a precise circular movement, signalling with her eyes for me to drip in the oil in a thin trickle. In less than five minutes, the bowl was full of unctuous mayonnaise. As a reward for having helped her to make it, I was allowed to lick the fork….. Sometimes she added a few snipped leaves of tarragon which she had bought in the market that very morning. She would place the herbs in a vase of water and keep them on the windowsill, just like a bunch of flowers. At The Waterside Inn, to bring pleasure to my customers, I have adopted the same principles of simplicity in my own approach to serving fish and shellfish.

I should like to remind my readers that there is no need to wash fish and shellfish in masses of water, still less to soak them for hours. It is enough to rinse them quickly under a trickle of cold water, then to dry them by dabbing delicately with a damp cloth. That way, you will preserve the firmness and texture of the flesh as well as the savour and aroma of this noble bounty from the sea.

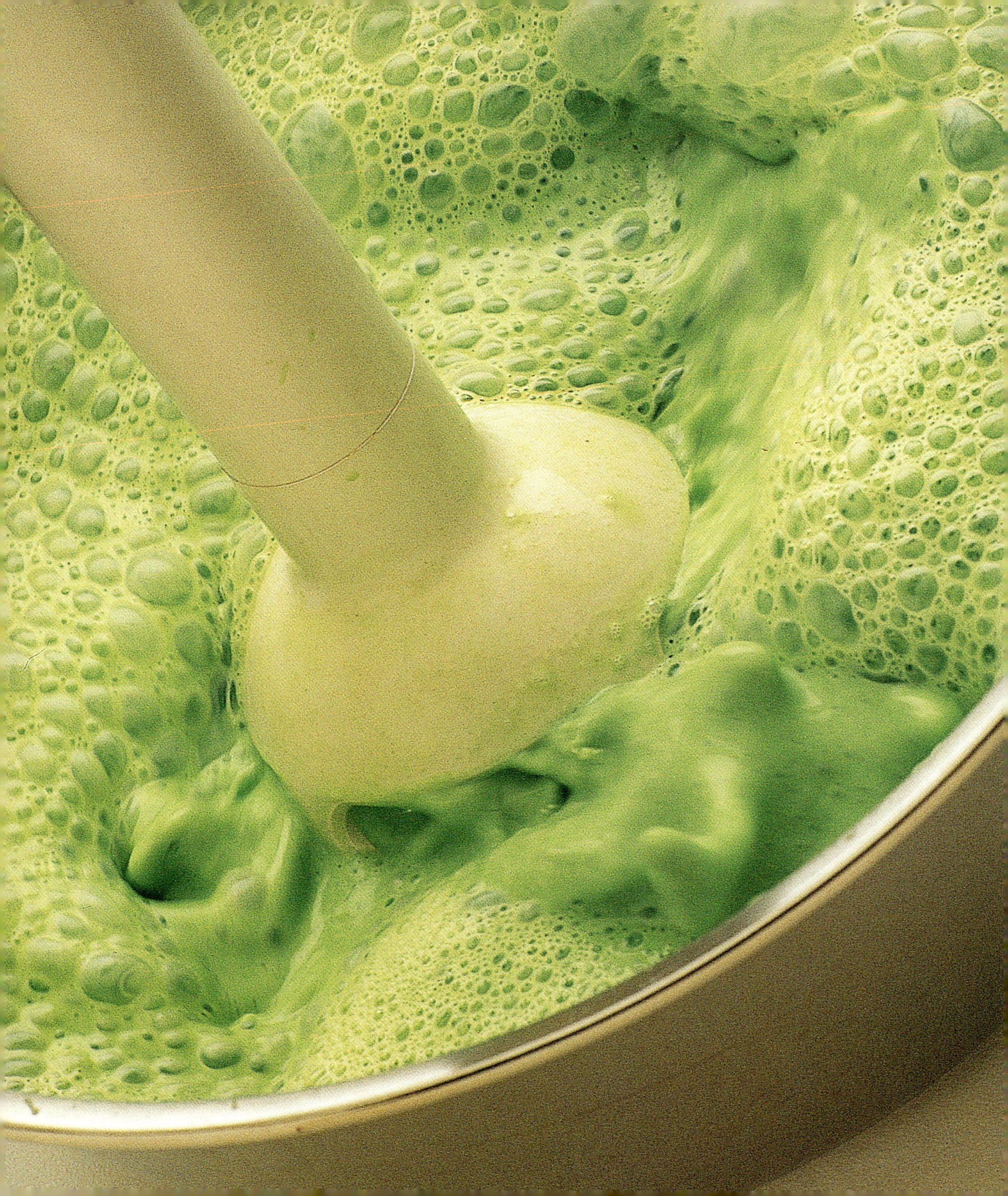

# About Sauces

In this book you will find sauces to suit every season, every taste and every occasion. Some are modern, some classic, some light, others unctuous, depending on the fish and shellfish they are destined to accompany. All are creative, delicious and not difficult to make at home.

- All sauces, however simple or complex, should be based on good quality ingredients. Aromatics, fresh herbs, spices, wines, spirits, stocks and fumets must all be chosen with the utmost care.
- In sauce-making, balance is all-important. It is vital to get the proportions exactly right, particularly in sauces for fish and shellfish, whose delicate flavour must be allowed to shine through. A sauce should provide the perfect accompaniment to a dish, but it should never dominate it.
- Very strong-flavoured ingredients like pungent spices, herbs and alcohol should always be used in moderation.

# Practical Advice

## *Menu Planning*

If you plan to serve more than one sauce at a meal, make only one elaborate or rich sauce and keep the others light and simple. Avoid serving sauces of the same colour and texture, and maintain a judicious balance between modern and classic sauces.

## *Techniques*

**Preparation time:** The preparation times given in this book are based on ingredients which have already been weighed out and prepared as indicated in the ingredients list. They do not include the time taken to peel, chop or slice vegetables or bones, soften butter, or any necessary cooling times.

**Cooking time:** The timings given are only guidelines, since the degree of heat will vary depending on your hob and the type of saucepan used. The only infallible way to check that a sauce has reached the desired consistency is to test it on the back of a spoon.

**Deglazing:** Wine or stock is heated with the cooking juices and sediment left in the pan after pan-frying to make a sauce. Pour off most of the fat or grease from the pan before adding the liquid.

**Straining:** Thin sauces can be passed straight through a conical sieve. Thicker sauces should be pushed through the sieve by pressing with the back of a ladle or twisting a small whisk.

**Keeping sauces warm:** A bain-marie or water bath is best for this. Use a saucepan large enough to hold the pan or bowl containing the sauce and fill it with hot water. Dot flakes of butter over the surface of white sauces to prevent a skin forming.

## *Dairy Products*

These play an extremely important part in sauce-making.

**Crème fraîche:** This can be successfully heated to not more than 80ºC; at higher temperatures, it will separate. To use it in a hot sauce, take the pan off the heat and whisk in the crème fraîche without further cooking.

**Double cream:** This tolerates heat extremely well during cooking and can even be reduced by boiling. It is often used as a liaison, but above all makes sauces creamy and velvety.

**Fromage blanc:** This is the champion of low-calorie sauces and is available in a virtually fat-free version. It is perfect for summer sauces, but its neutral taste demands the addition of flavourings like spices and herbs.

**Hard cheeses:** The most important and best are parmesan, gruyère, emmenthal and cheddar. I always use freshly grated medium-matured farmhouse cheeses which have a delicious full flavour. When adding cheese to a sauce, it takes a few minutes for the flavour to develop, so add it parsimoniously at first and check the development before adding more. Do not use cheap, poor quality cheeses, which can ruin a sauce by tasting rancid, soapy or too salty.

**Unsalted and clarified butter:** I use only unsalted butter in my cooking; it is better for all sauces and essential for making clarified butter. To make 100 g clarified butter, gently melt 120 g unsalted butter and bring slowly to the boil. Skim off the froth, then pour the melted butter into a bowl, leaving behind the milky sediment in the pan.

**Yoghurt:** I use tiny quantities of plain yoghurt to add a touch of acidity to certain sauces for fish.

## Flavourings and Seasoning

**Curry powder:** A pinch of curry powder added to foaming butter will enhance the flavour of steamed fish.

**Lemon and vinegar:** A few drops of lemon juice or vinegar added to a characterless sauce just before serving will pep it up.

**Saffron:** To obtain the maximum flavour when using saffron threads, pound them in a mortar or crush them with your fingertips into the palm of your hand, then infuse in a little warm water before using in recipes.

**Salt and pepper:** Do not add too much salt to a sauce before it has reached the desired consistency and taste. Add pepper only just before serving so that it retains its pungency.

**Shallots:** Shallots become bitter when chopped, so rinse them under cold water before using in a sauce.

**Shellfish cooking juices:** Keep the cooking juices from oysters, mussels, clams etc. A soon as possible after cooking the molluscs, add a small amount of strained cooking liquor to fish sauces to reinforce the flavour and make them more complex.

## Herbs and Spices

This subject deserves an entire encyclopaedia to do it justice, but since this is a book about sauces, I shall mention only those which I use to flavour and enhance my own cooking. If you use dried herbs, keep them in airtight jars in a cool, dark place. Spices lose their savour if they are kept too long; throw away any opened jars after 3 to 6 months because they will add nothing to your sauces and may even spoil them.

*TO MAKE A BOUQUET GARNI*
*Wrap the herbs in the leek leaf and tie up the bouquet garni with string*

*A classic bouquet garni consists of a sprig of thyme, a bay leaf, parsley stalks and a leek leaf*

**Fines herbes:** A mixture of fresh herbs in equal quantities: chervil, chives, parsley and tarragon. They should be snipped, not chopped, only just before using to retain the maximum flavour and stop them becoming bitter.

## The golden rules for using herbs and spices

- Go for quality rather than quantity when using herbs and spices; small quantities are usually enough
- Do not mix contradictory and powerful flavours

If you obey these rules, you will discover a wonderful world of flavours – subtle, complex, musky, fresh, spicy and utterly delectable.

# Vegetable Stock or Nage

*Nages are light aromatic poaching stocks, and I like to add a hint of acidity to mine, hence the vinegar. I don't, however, use vinegar in my classic vegetable stock. You can substitute or add your own choice of seasonal vegetables, varying the stock with nice ripe tomatoes in summer, a few wild mushrooms in autumn (chanterelles add a particularly fine aroma), and so on.*

### Ingredients:

300 g carrots, cut into rounds
White part of 2 leeks, thinly sliced
100 g celery stalks, thinly sliced
50 g bulb fennel, very thinly sliced
150 g shallots, thinly sliced
100 g onion, thinly sliced
2 unpeeled garlic cloves
1 bouquet garni (page 9)
250 ml dry white wine
2 L water
10 white peppercorns, crushed and wrapped in a piece of muslin
3 tbsp white wine vinegar (only for a nage)

Makes 1.5 litres
Preparation time: **15 minutes**
Cooking time: **45 minutes**

Put all the ingredients except the peppercorns in a saucepan (1). Bring to the boil over high heat, then cook at a bare simmer for 45 minutes, skimming as necessary (2). After 35 minutes, add the muslin-wrapped peppercorns. Strain through a fine-mesh conical sieve into a bowl (3). Cool the stock as quickly as possible (see below).

### Cooling and freezing stocks

In the restaurant I cool my strained stocks very rapidly using a blast freezer to prevent the spread of bacteria. At home, I fill a container with ice cubes and plunge in the pan or bowl of boiling stock, which cools quite quickly. As soon as the stock is cold, I put it in airtight containers, keeping what I need in the fridge and freezing the rest. All stocks will keep in the fridge for several days, or in the freezer for up to four weeks.

❸

12  Stocks

# Fish Stock or Fumet

*Fish stock can be used as the base for an aspic to serve with cold fish. Just add a few gelatine leaves and season with salt and pepper before the gelatine sets. If you intend to use the stock for a red wine sauce, substitute red wine for the white when making the stock.*

**Ingredients:**

1.5 kg bones and trimmings of white fish (eg sole, turbot, brill, whiting), cut into pieces
50 g butter
White of 2 leeks, thinly sliced
75 g onions, thinly sliced
75 g button mushrooms, thinly sliced
200 ml dry white wine
1 bouquet garni (page 9)
2 slices of lemon
8 white peppercorns, crushed and wrapped in a piece of muslin

*Makes 2 litres*
*Preparation time:* **20 minutes**
*Cooking time:* **about 30 minutes**

Rinse the fish bones and trimmings under cold running water, then drain (1). In a saucepan, melt the butter and sweat the vegetables over low heat for a few minutes. Add the fish bones and trimmings (2), bubble gently for a few moments, then pour in the wine (3). Cook until it has evaporated by two-thirds, then add 2.5 litres cold water (4). Bring to the boil, lower the heat, skim the surface (5) and add the bouquet garni and lemon. Simmer very gently for 25 minutes, skimming as necessary. 10 minutes before the end of cooking, add the muslin-wrapped peppercorns (6). Gently pour or ladle the stock through a fine-mesh conical sieve (7) and cool it as quickly as possible (see page 10).

**Fish velouté:** For an excellent fish velouté, add 60 g white roux (page 14) per litre of stock and cook for 20 minutes.

# White Roux

*This roux is classically used as a thickener in all white sauces.*

**Ingredients:** Makes 100 g
50 g butter — Preparation time: **3 minutes**
50 g flour, sifted — Cooking time: **4 minutes**

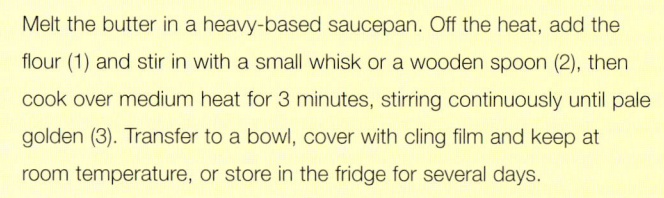

Melt the butter in a heavy-based saucepan. Off the heat, add the flour (1) and stir in with a small whisk or a wooden spoon (2), then cook over medium heat for 3 minutes, stirring continuously until pale golden (3). Transfer to a bowl, cover with cling film and keep at room temperature, or store in the fridge for several days.

# Blond Roux

*This pale roux is used to thicken veloutés and sauces where a neutral colour is required, particularly those for white fish.*

**Ingredients:** Makes 100 g
50 g butter — Preparation time: **3 minutes**
50 g flour, sifted — Cooking time: **6 minutes**

Melt the butter in a heavy-based saucepan. Off the heat, add the flour (1) and stir in with a small whisk or a wooden spoon (2), then cook over medium heat for 5 minutes, stirring continuously. The roux should be a rich golden colour (4). Transfer to a bowl, cover with cling film and keep at room temperature, or store in the fridge for several days.

# Mayonnaise

*Mayonnaise forms the basis for numerous other sauces. It is also delicious served just as it is with cold crab, lobster and langoustines, or poached fish such as salmon, hake and cod; the list is endless.*

*If you prefer, you can replace some of the groundnut oil with olive oil, but do not use more than one-quarter, as olive oil has a very pronounced flavour. For a creamier mayonnaise, mix in 2 tablespoons double cream after adding the warm vinegar or cold lemon juice.*

**Ingredients:** Serves 4
2 egg yolks
1 tbsp strong Dijon mustard
250 ml groundnut oil
1 tbsp white wine vinegar, warmed, or
1 tbsp cold lemon juice
Salt and freshly ground pepper

Preparation time: **5 minutes**

Lay a tea towel on the work surface and stand a mixing or salad bowl on the towel. In the bowl, combine the egg yolks, mustard and a little salt and pepper and mix with a whisk. Pour in the oil in a thin, steady stream, whisking continuously. When it is all incorporated, whisk more vigorously for 30 seconds to make a thick, glossy mayonnaise, then add the hot vinegar or cold lemon juice. Adjust the seasoning with salt and pepper.

The mayonnaise can be kept at room temperature, covered with cling film, until ready to use. However, it is not wise to keep it for more than a few hours unless you use pasteurized eggs.

*Mayonnaise makes a wonderful dip for crustaceans*

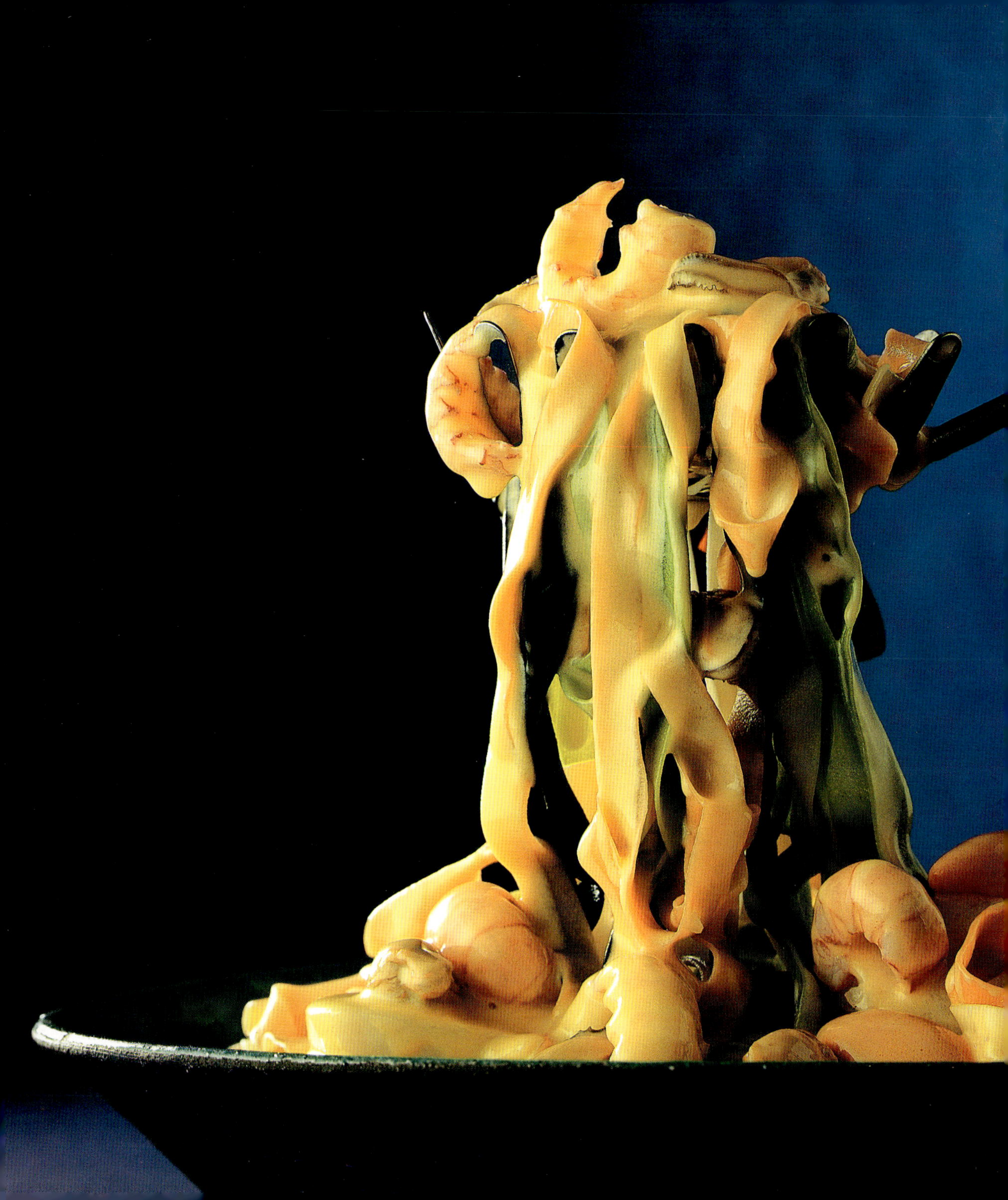

# Recipes

- Sauces for fish should be delicate and light; their flavour should harmonize with the seafood they accompany and never dominate it. This is particularly important in the case of white fish. I like to serve fish with a nage, a light, aromatic stock, to which I sometimes add just a tiny soupçon of fresh herbs, like snipped chervil, basil or tarragon.
- I prefer my fish barely cooked, so that it remains juicy. The sauce should be there to bring out the fresh, salty tang and the delicate flavour of the sea, adding extra pleasure to the palate.
- In contrast, sauces for crustaceans should be flavoured with stronger herbs and spices to give them a more defined edge and character.
- Sauces for fish and seafood often contain dry white wine; variations include beer, champagne, vermouth or even a sweet sauternes.

*Tagliatelle and Seafood Sauce with Saffron (page 28)*

# Fromage Blanc Sauce with Curry

Use this sauce as a dressing for a summer salad of green beans, new potatoes or crudités, or with cold cooked mussels. You can adjust the quantity of curry slightly to suit your own taste, or even substitute 15 g fresh mint, which you infuse in the milk. This version is delicious with cold pasta and a scattering of shredded mint leaves.

**Ingredients:**
100 ml milk
1 tbsp curry powder
300 g fromage blanc (whichever fat content you prefer)
Salt and freshly ground pepper

Serves 6
Preparation time: **3 minutes**
Cooking time: **2 minutes, plus cooling**

In a small saucepan, bring the milk to the boil. Add the curry, simmer for 2 minutes, then leave at room temperature to cool completely. Strain the cold curry-flavoured milk through a wire-mesh sieve, then stir it into the fromage blanc. Season to taste with salt and pepper. The sauce is now ready to use.

# Yoghurt Sauce

This simple refreshing sauce is excellent with all cold vegetables, cold pasta and hard-boiled eggs as well as with fish. It is very quick to make.

**Ingredients:**
600 ml plain yoghurt
100 g Mayonnaise (see page 15)
2 tbsp snipped fresh herbs of your choice (eg chervil, parsley, chives, tarragon)
1 medium marmande tomato, peeled (page 34), deseeded and diced
A small pinch of cayenne pepper, or 4 drops of tabasco
Salt

Serves 8
Preparation time: **10 minutes**

Mix all the ingredients together and, voilà, your sauce is ready to serve.

# Fresh Goat's Cheese Sauce with Rosemary

*Serve this sauce with a basket of crudités, cold poached fish, roast or poached chicken, or with large shrimps or prawns.*

**Ingredients:**

250 ml milk (if the cheese has a very soft consistency, you may need only 150 – 200 ml)
30 g fresh rosemary needles
300 g fresh goat's cheese, softened with a spatula
Salt and freshly ground pepper

Serves 6
Preparation time: **3 minutes**
Cooking time: **2 minutes, plus cooling**

In a small saucepan, bring the milk to the boil. Add the rosemary needles, cover the pan and leave to infuse until completely cold. Strain the cooled milk, whisk it into the goat's cheese and season to taste with salt and pepper. The sauce is now ready to serve.

# Fishbone Sauce

*This sauce is quick to prepare, light and full of flavour. It goes very well with poached fish or steamed scallops.*

**Ingredients:**

150 g butter, diced
40 g shallots, chopped
200 g white fish bones (eg sole or turbot), roughly chopped
100 ml dry white wine
100 ml cold water
1 sprig of thyme
A few drops of lemon juice
Salt and freshly ground pepper

Serves 4
Preparation time: **10 minutes**
Cooking time: **10 minutes**

Melt 50 g butter in a small saucepan. Add the shallots and fishbones, and sweat gently for 3 minutes, stirring with a wooden spoon. Pour in the wine and cook for 2 minutes. Add the water and thyme and bubble for 3 minutes, then skim the surface if necessary. Toss in the remaining butter, one piece at a time, rotating the pan and swirling it about to incorporate the butter, then add the lemon juice. Season to taste with salt and pepper and pass the sauce through a wire-mesh conical sieve. It is now ready to use.

# Asparagus Coulis

*This delicious sauce is almost as light as a nage. I add some asparagus tips at the last moment and serve it with delicate steamed fish, or pour it around my vegetable lasagne to make a dish which even non-vegetarians love.*

**Ingredients:**

350 g asparagus spears, preferably small ones
50 g butter
80 g shallots, chopped
1 sprig of thyme
300 ml Vegetable Stock (page 10), chicken stock or water
500 ml double cream
1 tsp soy sauce (optional)
Salt and freshly ground pepper

Serves 8
Preparation time: **10 minutes**
Cooking time: **about 40 minutes**

Peel the asparagus stalks with a vegetable peeler. Cut off the tips and blanch them in boiling salted water. Refresh, drain and set aside. Chop the stalks and leave them raw. In a thick-bottomed saucepan, melt the butter, add the chopped asparagus stalks and shallots and sweat gently for 5 minutes. Add the thyme and the stock or water and cook over medium heat for 15 minutes. Pour in the cream, increase the heat to high and reduce the coulis by one-third. Whizz in a blender for 3 minutes, then pass through a conical sieve. Season with to taste, adding the reserved asparagus tips and the soy sauce if you wish. Keep the coulis warm until needed.

# Light Carrot Coulis

*This coulis is almost like a jus and should be eaten with a spoon. It goes well with pan-fried scallops, grilled white fish and also with rice pilaff.*

**Ingredients:**

3 carrots, total weight about 250 g
Juice of 2 oranges
200 ml Vegetable Stock (page 10) or veal stock
1 tsp freshly grated ginger
60 g butter, chilled and diced
Salt and freshly ground pepper

Serves 6
Preparation time: **5 minutes**
Cooking time: **about 10 minutes**

Peel the carrots, cut them into small pieces, then whizz them in a food processor with the orange juice and stock for 3 minutes. Transfer to a saucepan, set over high heat and reduce the coulis for about 10 minutes, until it lightly coats the back of a spoon. Add the ginger, take the pan off the heat, and whisk in the butter, a little at a time. Season to taste, pass through a conical sieve and serve.

# Leek Coulis with Curry

*Spread a spoonful of this coulis over individual plates and top with grilled or pan-fried firm-fleshed fish such as monkfish or turbot, or some langoustines à la meunière.*

**Ingredients:**
500 g tender small or medium leeks
40 g butter
$1/2$ tsp curry powder
250 ml Vegetable Stock (page 10) or chicken stock
300 ml double cream
$1/2$ tsp mustard powder
Salt and freshly ground pepper

Serves 8
Preparation time: **10 minutes**
Cooking time: **about 40 minutes**

Cut off the greenest parts of the leeks and the root ends. Split the leeks lengthways, wash meticulously in cold water, then slice them finely. Blanch in boiling, salted water, refresh and drain.

In a thick-bottomed saucepan, melt the butter and sweat the leeks gently for 10 minutes. Add the curry powder, then the stock and cook over medium heat for 10 minutes. Add the cream and mustard powder and simmer for a further 10 minutes, then whizz in a blender for 5 minutes. Pass the coulis through a conical sieve back into the pan. Season and keep the coulis warm, without letting it boil, until ready to serve.

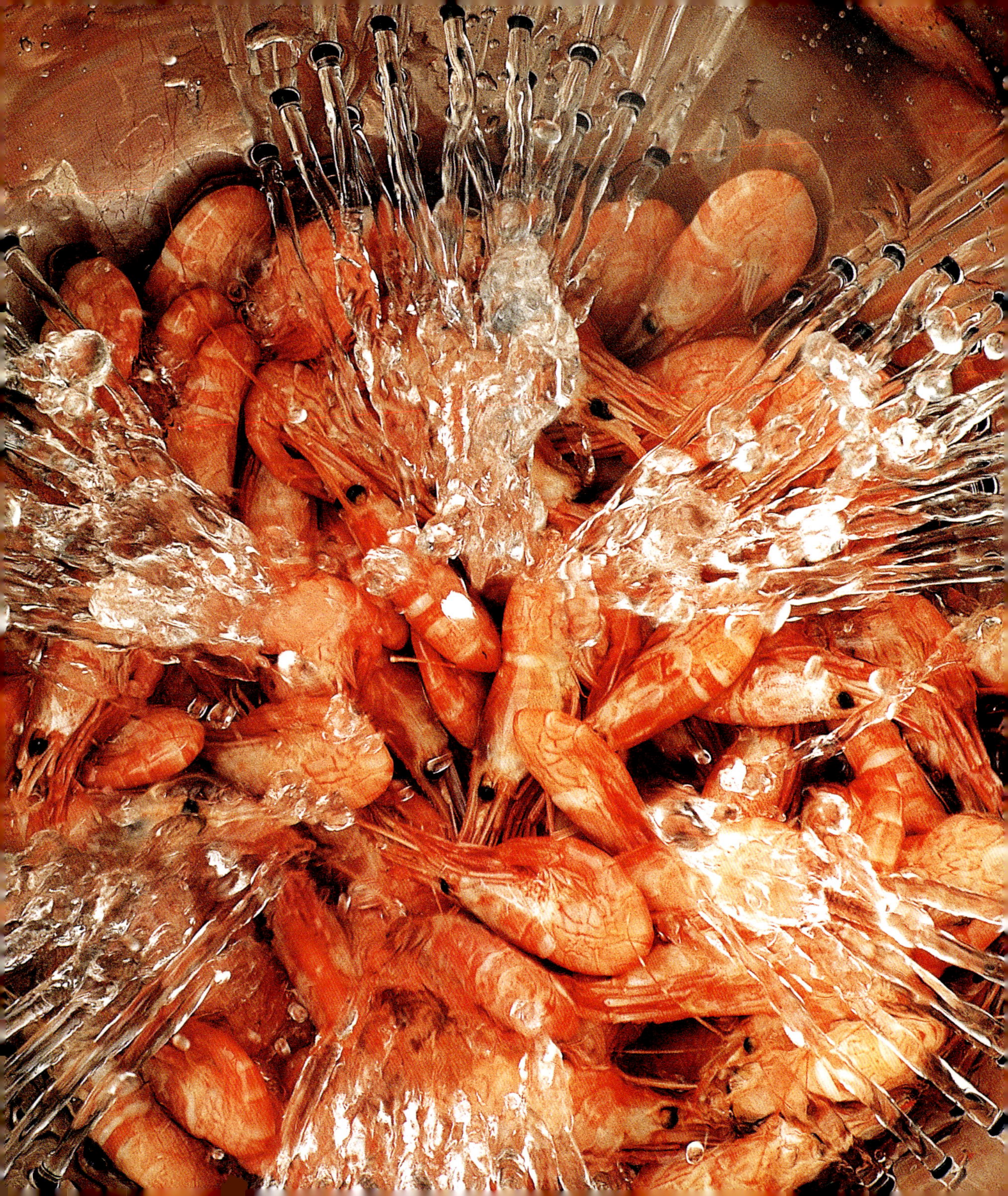

# Shrimp Butter

*Discs of shrimp butter add a special something to pan-fried or grilled fish. It can be used to enrich a fish sauce, or served as canapés spread on toasted croûtons. For extra zing, add a pinch of cayenne pepper.*

**Ingredients:**

150 g very fresh pink or brown shrimps

150 g butter, softened

Cayenne pepper (optional)

*Makes about 220 g*

*Preparation time:* **10 minutes**

Rinse the shrimps in cold water, leaving any eggs attached, drain and pat dry in a tea towel.

Place the shrimps in a blender with the butter and a pinch of cayenne, if you like (1). Process for about 3 minutes, scraping the ingredients into the centre of the bowl every minute, to obtain a homogeneous mixture (2). If you prefer, you can use a pestle and mortar instead of a blender.

Using a plastic scraper, rub the flavoured butter through a drum sieve to eliminate the shrimp shells (3). Using cling film, roll the butter into one or two sausage shapes and refrigerate or freeze until ready to slice and serve.

**Pan-fried fish topped with Shrimp Butter**

# Langoustine Butter

*Enrich fish sauces with this butter. It also makes wonderful canapés spread on toast croûtons and topped with langoustine tails.*

**Ingredients:**

50 g butter, preferably clarified (page 8)
1 small carrot, finely diced
1 medium onion, finely diced
12 crayfish or langoustines, live if possible
5 tbsp cognac or armagnac
200 ml white wine
1 small bouquet garni (page 9)
2 pinches of cayenne pepper
Softened butter, 75% of the weight of the cooked crustacean heads and claws
Salt and freshly ground pepper

Makes about 500 g
Preparation time: **15 minutes**
Cooking time: **about 20 minutes**

Melt the butter in a deep frying pan, add the diced carrot and onion and sweat until soft. Using a slotted spoon, transfer the vegetables to a ramekin, leaving the cooking butter in the pan.

Put the crustaceans in the pan and sauté over high heat for 2 minutes. Add the Cognac, ignite it, then moisten with the white wine. Add the cooked diced vegetables, bouquet garni, a little cayenne and a small pinch of salt and cook gently over low heat for 10 minutes. Tip all the contents of the pan into a bowl and leave to cool completely at room temperature.

To make the flavoured butter, separate the crayfish or langoustine heads and tails. Keep the tails for another use (as an hors d'oeuvre salad or canapés, for example). Gather up the heads and claws, and the creamy flesh from the heads and weigh them. Place in a food processor or blender with 75% of their weight of softened butter and the diced vegetables, and whizz until mushy. Rub through a drum sieve with a plastic scraper and season to taste. Using cling film, roll the flavoured butter into one or two sausage shapes and refrigerate or freeze until needed.

# Pistachio Butter

*I use this butter in my Sauternes Sauce with Pistachios (page 44) or add it to a Hollandaise (page 49) to give a touch of mellowness.*

**Ingredients:**

100 g raw skinned pistachio nuts
1 tbsp water
150 g butter, softened
Salt and freshly ground pepper

*Makes about 250 g*
*Preparation time: 7 minutes*

Pound the pistachios to a paste with the water in a mortar or food processor. Add all the butter at once, mix and season, then rub through a drum sieve with a plastic scraper. Using cling film, roll the pistachio butter into one or two sausage shapes and refrigerate or freeze until ready to use.

# Anchovy Butter

*Use this delicious butter on grilled fish, or serve it on toast canapés topped with a julienne of anchovy fillets.*

**Ingredients:**

50 g anchovy fillets in oil
150 g butter, softened
Salt and freshly ground pepper

*Makes about 180 g*
*Preparation time: 7 minutes*

Chop the anchovy fillets or pound them in a mortar. Using a wooden spoon, mix them into the butter and, using a plastic scraper, rub through a drum sieve or whizz in a food processor. Season, being circumspect with the salt, as the anchovies already contain plenty. Use cling film to roll the butter into one or two sausage shapes and refrigerate or freeze until ready to use.

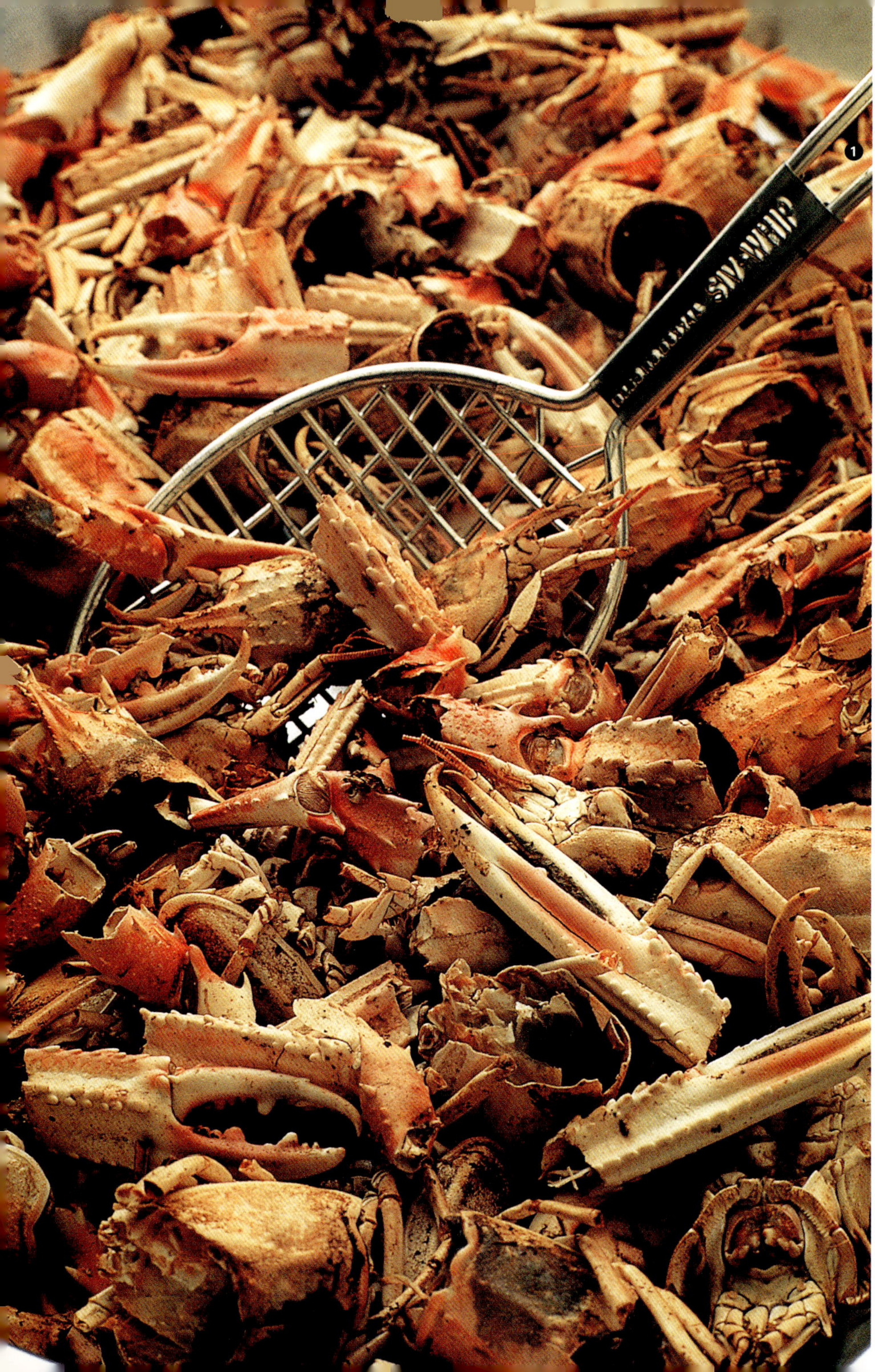
1

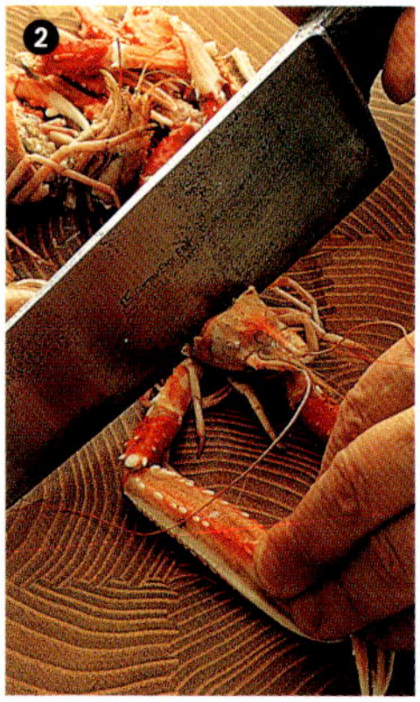
2

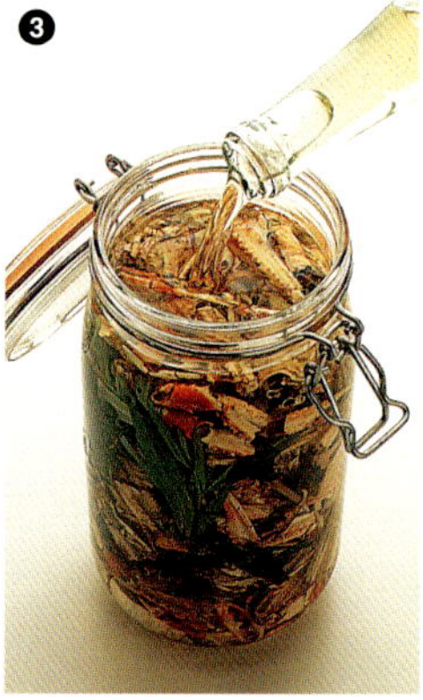
3

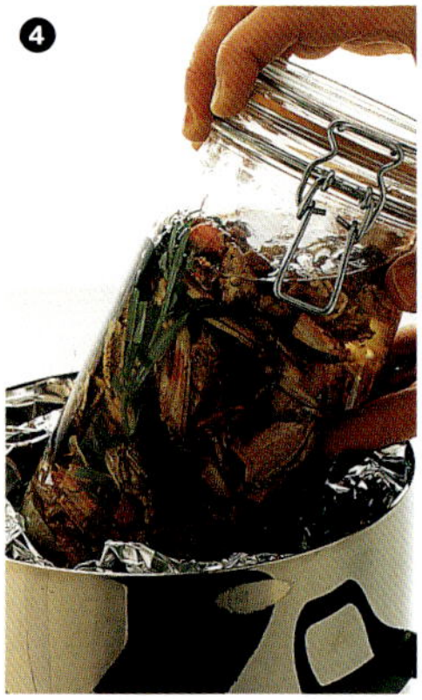
4

# Crustacean Oil

*This wonderfully delicate oil is one of my favourites. It makes a superb dressing for fantasy seafood salads or warm asparagus spears.*

**Ingredients:**

1 kg langoustines or crayfish, cooked in salted water
1/2 head of garlic, unpeeled
1 sprig of thyme
2 bay leaves
1 small bunch of tarragon
1 tsp whole white peppercorns
1/2 tsp whole coriander seeds
Approximately 1 L groundnut or olive oil
Salt

**Special equipment:**

A 1 – 1.5 L kilner jar. Ideally, this should be new – if not, it must be scrupulously clean

Makes about 1 litre
Preparation time: *20 minutes, plus 3 hours' drying*
Sterilization time: *35 – 45 minutes*

Preheat the oven to 120°C/250°F/gas mark 1/2. Remove the eyes of the crustaceans and separate the heads, claws and tails (1). Keep the tails to use as a garnish for fish or serve in a salad as an hors d'oeuvre. Roughly chop the heads and claws with a chef's knife (2), put them in a roasting pan and place in the oven to dry for 3 hours. Put the dried heads and claws into the kilner jar with the aromatics, fill up with oil to within 2 cm of the top (3) and seal the lid carefully.

To sterilize the oil, you will need a saucepan at least as tall as the jar. Line the bottom and sides of the pan with foil; this will protect the glass, which might explode if it should knock against the side of the pan. Put in the jar (4) and pour in enough water salted with 300 g salt per litre of water to come up to the level of the oil in the jar, but not to submerge it. Bring the water to the boil over high heat and boil for 35 to 45 minutes, depending on the size of the kilner jar.

After sterilization, leave the jar at room temperature until completely cold, then refrigerate for at least 8 days before using the oil. It will keep for months in the sealed sterile jar if stored in a cool place. Once opened, decant the oil into a bottle; it will keep for several weeks in the fridge.

# Seafood Sauce with Saffron

This is the perfect sauce for any lightly poached seafood, langoustines or lobster, or for fresh flat pasta (picture page 16).

**Ingredients:**
350 ml cooking juices from shellfish, such as mussels, scallops, oysters, clams etc
250 ml Fish Stock (page 13), or cooking juices from langoustines
A pinch of saffron threads
200 ml double cream
Salt and freshly ground white pepper

Serves 4
Preparation time: **10 minutes**
Cooking time: **about 20 minutes**

Combine the shellfish juices and fish stock in a saucepan, set over high heat and reduce by two-thirds. Add the saffron and cream and bubble for 5 minutes, until the sauce will lightly coat the back of a spoon. Pass it through a conical sieve and season to taste. For a less calorific sauce, you can substitute fromage frais for the double cream, but do not allow the sauce to boil. Heat it to 90°C and whisk well before serving, or, better still, give it a quick whizz in a blender.

# Champagne Sauce

This sauce is perfect for poached white fish, such as John Dory, turbot or sole. You can substitute sparkling white wine for the champagne, but the sauce will not taste as good.

**Ingredients:**
50 g butter
60 g shallots, very finely sliced
60 g button mushrooms, finely sliced
400 ml brut champagne
300 ml Fish Stock (page 13)
500 ml double cream
Salt and freshly ground white pepper

Serves 8
Preparation time: **10 minutes**
Cooking time: **about 50 minutes**

In a saucepan, melt 20 g butter. Add the shallots and sweat them for 1 minute, without colouring. Add the mushrooms and cook for a further 2 minutes, stirring continuously with a wooden spatula. Pour in the champagne and reduce by one-third over medium heat. Add the fish stock and reduce the sauce by half.

Pour in the cream and reduce the sauce until it lightly coats the back of a spoon. Pass it through a fine-mesh conical sieve into a clean pan. Whisk in the remaining butter, a little at a time, then season the sauce with salt and pepper. For a lighter texture, whizz the sauce in a food processor for 1 minute before serving.

# Nantua Sauce

*An excellent sauce for langoustines, scallops and any white fish with delicate, firm flesh. A tablespoon of snipped tarragon added just before serving will make it taste even better.*

**Ingredients:**

120 g butter
60 g shallots, very finely sliced
60 g button mushrooms, very finely sliced
16 crayfish or langoustine heads, raw or cooked, roughly chopped
2 tbsp cognac
150 ml dry white wine
300 ml Fish Stock (page 13)
1 small bouquet garni (page 9), including a sprig or two of tarragon
80 g ripe tomatoes, peeled (page 34) and deseeded
A pinch of cayenne pepper
300 ml double cream
Salt and freshly ground pepper

Serves 8
Preparation time: **20 minutes**
Cooking time: **about 50 minutes**

In a shallow saucepan, melt 40 g butter over low heat. Add the shallots and mushrooms and sweat for 1 minute. Add the crayfish or langoustine heads to the pan, increase the heat and fry briskly for 2 – 3 minutes, stirring continuously with a spatula.

Pour in the cognac, ignite with a match, add the wine and reduce by half, then pour in the fish stock. Bring to the boil, then lower the heat so that the sauce bubbles gently. Add the bouquet garni, tomato, cayenne and a smidgeon of salt and cook for 30 minutes.

Stir in the cream and bubble the sauce for another 10 minutes. Remove the bouquet garni, transfer the contents of the pan to a food processor and whizz for 2 minutes. Strain the sauce through a fine-mesh conical sieve into a clean saucepan, rubbing it through with the back of a ladle. Bring the sauce back to the boil and season with salt and pepper. Off the heat, whisk in the remaining butter, a little at a time, until the sauce is smooth and glossy. It is now ready to serve.

# Américaine Sauce

*This classic 'star' takes time to prepare, but is worth the effort. Serve it with firm-fleshed fish, such as poached turbot.*

Serves 6
Preparation time: **40 minutes**
Cooking time: **about 1 hour**

### Ingredients:

1 live lobster, 800 g – 1 kg
100 ml groundnut oil
4 tbsp very finely diced carrots
2 tbsp very finely diced shallot or onion
2 garlic cloves, unpeeled and crushed
50 ml cognac or armagnac
300 ml dry white wine
300 ml Fish Stock (page 13)
200 g very ripe tomatoes, peeled (page 34), deseeded and chopped
1 bouquet garni (page 9), containing a sprig of tarragon
60 g butter
10 g flour
A small pinch of cayenne pepper
75 ml double cream (optional)
Salt and freshly ground pepper

Bring a large pan of water to the boil. Rinse the lobster under cold running water and plunge it into the boiling water for 45 seconds. Separate the head and body and cut the claw joints and tail into rings across the articulations (1). Split the head lengthways and remove the gritty sac close to the feelers (2), and the dirty white membranes. Scrape out the greenish coral from inside the head (3) and reserve in a bowl. Season the lobster with cayenne, salt and pepper.

In a deep frying pan or shallow saucepan, heat the oil over high heat. As soon as it is sizzling hot, add all the lobster pieces (4) and sauté until the shell turns bright red and the flesh is lightly coloured (5). Remove the lobster pieces with a slotted spoon (6) and place on a plate. Discard most of the cooking oil.

Using the same pan, sweat the carrot and shallot until soft but not coloured. Add the garlic, return the lobster pieces to the pan, pour in the cognac or

Sauces for Fish and Shellfish

armagnac and light with a match. Add the wine and fish stock, then add the tomatoes, bouquet garni and a touch of salt. As soon as the mixture comes to the boil, lower the heat and cook gently for 15 minutes. Remove and reserve the claws and rings of lobster tail containing the meat. Cook the sauce at a gentle bubble for a further 30 minutes, skimming it every 15 minutes.

Using a fork, mash together the reserved lobster coral, butter and flour, and add this mixture to the sauce, a little at a time (7). Cook for another 5 minutes, then add the cream if you wish and pass the sauce through a fine-mesh conical strainer, pressing it through with the back of a ladle (8). Season with salt and pepper. For a lighter texture, whizz the sauce in a food processor for 1 minute. Remove the reserved lobster meat from the shell, dice it and add to the sauce just before serving.

# Claret Sauce

*Serve this vinous, characterful sauce as a base for pan-fried pink-fleshed fish, such as salmon, red mullet or tuna escalopes. For a fuller flavour, use 200 ml veal stock and 300 ml fish stock.*

**Ingredients:**

300 ml full-bodied red wine
500 ml Fish Stock (page 13), made with red wine
50 g shallots, finely sliced
60 g button mushrooms, finely sliced
1 small bouquet garni (page 9)
50 ml double cream
200 g butter, chilled and diced
Salt and freshly ground pepper

Serves 8
Preparation time: **5 minutes**
Cooking time: **about 40 minutes**

Combine all the ingredients except the cream and butter in a saucepan, set over medium heat and reduce until slightly syrupy. Remove the bouquet garni, add the cream and give the sauce a good bubble, then strain it through a conical sieve into a clean saucepan. Whisk in the butter, a small piece at a time, until the sauce is rich and glossy. Season to taste and serve hot.

# Bercy Sauce

*This simple, classic sauce goes well with any red- or white-fleshed fish. I enjoy it served with an unusual fish, roussette (dogfish or huss) and also with skate.*

**Ingredients:**

60 g butter
60 g shallots, very finely chopped
200 ml dry white wine
150 ml Fish Stock (page 13)
400 ml Fish Velouté (page 13)
Juice of $1/2$ lemon
2 tbsp snipped parsley, or 1 tbsp snipped tarragon
Salt and freshly ground pepper

Serves 6
Preparation time: **10 minutes**
Cooking time: **about 35 minutes**

Melt 20 g butter in a saucepan, add the shallots and sweat them gently for 1 minute. Pour in the wine and fish stock and cook over medium heat until the liquid has reduced by half. Add the fish velouté and simmer gently for 20 minutes. The sauce should be thick enough to coat the back of a spoon lightly. If it is not, cook it for a further 5 – 10 minutes. Turn off the heat and whisk in the remaining butter and the lemon juice. Season the sauce, stir in the snipped parsley or tarragon and serve immediately.

# Tomato Nage

*This light nage is perfect with lightly poached crustaceans, or grilled fish such as escalope of salmon or fillets of sole.*

**Ingredients:**

350 g very ripe tomatoes, peeled (page 34), deseeded and chopped
1 tsp tomato purée (optional)
50 g shallots, finely sliced
50 g button mushrooms, finely sliced
1 sprig of thyme
1 bay leaf
250 ml Vegetable Stock (page 10)
A pinch of sugar
50 ml double cream
250 g butter
Salt and freshly ground pepper

Serves 8
Preparation time: **15 minutes**
Cooking time: **25 minutes**

Combine all the ingredients except the cream and butter in a saucepan and bring to the boil over medium heat. As soon as the mixture starts to bubble, lower the heat and reduce the liquid by two-thirds. Now add the cream and bubble the sauce for 3 minutes. Off the heat, whisk in the butter, a little at a time. Strain the sauce through a fine-mesh conical sieve into a clean saucepan and season to taste. The nage is now ready to use.

If the tomatoes are slightly lacking in flavour, add a teaspoon of tomato purée.

# Fish Fumet with Tomatoes

*This summery, fat-free sauce is delicious ladled over steamed fillets of fish like red mullet, John Dory or sea bream.*

**Ingredients:**

600 ml Fish Stock (page 13)
500 g very ripe tomatoes, chopped
1 small red pepper, white membranes and seeds removed, very thinly sliced
50 g basil, snipped
4 egg whites
8 peppercorns, crushed
Salt and freshly ground pepper

Serves 6
Preparation time: **5 minutes**
Cooking time: **about 30 minutes**

First make the clarification mixture which will make the fumet crystal clear.. Thoroughly mix together all the ingredients except the fish stock. Pour the fish stock into a saucepan and add the clarification mixture. Bring to the boil over medium heat, stirring every 5 minutes with a wooden spoon. As soon as the liquid boils, reduce the heat and bubble very gently for 20 minutes. Pass the clarified fumet through a wire-mesh conical sieve, season with salt and pepper and serve.

**How to peel tomatoes:** Cut a cross in the top of the tomatoes and gouge out the cores. Drop the tomatoes into boiling water until the skin starts to split (about 10 – 20 seconds) then take them out and plunge them into iced water. Lift out the tomatoes with a draining spoon and slip off the skins.

# Cooked Tomato Coulis

This tomato coulis is extremely versatile, and I use it frequently in my kitchen. It is divine spread over a plate and topped with grilled fish. Alternatively add a small quantity to a fish sauce, or, better still, a Béchamel Sauce (page 58).

Serves 4
Preparation time: 5 minutes
Cooking time: about 1 hour

**Ingredients:**
150 ml olive oil
2 garlic cloves, crushed
60 g shallots, finely chopped
1 small bouquet garni (page 9), containing plenty of thyme
750 g very ripe marmande tomatoes, peeled (opposite), deseeded and chopped
1 tbsp tomato purée (only if the tomatoes are not ripe enough)
A pinch of sugar
6 peppercorns, crushed
Salt

In a thick-bottomed saucepan, warm the olive oil with the garlic, shallots and bouquet garni. After 2 minutes, add the tomatoes (1), tomato purée if needed, sugar and crushed peppercorns, and cook very gently for about 1 hour, stirring occasionally with a wooden spoon until all the moisture has evaporated (2). Remove the bouquet garni and whizz the contents of the pan in a blender to make a smooth purée (3). Season to taste. The coulis is ready to use immediately, but you can keep it in an airtight container in the fridge for five days.

If the sauce is to be served plain, after reheating, add a little olive oil just before serving.

# Mandarin Sauce

This sauce glows with colour and warmth and is particularly good in autumn or winter. Its delicious gentle flavour makes it ideal with poached white-fleshed fish. I serve it with paupiettes of sole, simply poached or filled with a lobster mousse.

*Serves 4*
Preparation time: **7 minutes**
Cooking time: **about 20 minutes**

### Ingredients:

*250 g peeled mandarins, segmented*
*150 ml Fish Stock (page 13)*
*150 ml double cream*
*2 tbsp Napoléon mandarine liqueur or grand marnier*
*Zest of 1 mandarin, cut into julienne and blanched (optional)*
*60 g butter, chilled and diced*
*Salt and freshly ground pepper*

Put the mandarin segments in a food processor, mix to a pulp and rub through a fine-mesh sieve. Pour the resulting mandarin juice and the fish stock into a small saucepan, set over medium heat and reduce by half. Add the cream and liqueur and bubble the sauce for a few minutes, until it lightly coats the back of a spoon. Pass it again through the conical sieve. Off the heat, whisk in the butter, a little at a time, to make a smooth shiny sauce. Season to taste, then add the mandarin zest if you wish. Serve at once.

**Paupiettes of sole filled with lobster mousse, served with Mandarin Sauce**

# Parsley Nage with Lemon Grass

*This light, fresh sauce has a gentle lemony flavour underlying the delicious aroma of parsley. Serve it with any poached or pan-fried fish, or with scallops and langoustines.*

**Ingredients:**

100 g flat-leaf parsley, stalks and leaves coarsely chopped
30 g shallot, chopped
1 lemon grass stalk, split lengthways
300 ml Fish Stock (page 13) or Vegetable Stock (page 10)
4 tbsp double cream
Juice of ½ lemon
200 g butter, chilled and diced
2 tbsp finely snipped parsley leaves
Salt and freshly ground pepper

*Serves 6*
*Preparation time:* **10 minutes**
*Cooking time:* **about 30 minutes**

Put the chopped parsley, shallot, lemon grass and stock in a saucepan and cook very gently for 10 minutes. Remove the lemon grass, transfer the contents of the pan to a blender and purée for 1 minute. Pass the purée through a wire-mesh conical sieve into a clean saucepan, add the cream and lemon juice and bring to the boil. Bubble until the sauce is just thick enough to coat the back of a spoon very lightly. Reduce the heat to as low as possible and incorporate the butter, a little at a time, whisking continuously. Season the sauce to taste with salt and pepper, stir in the finely snipped parsley and serve at once.

# Watercress Sauce

*A tasty sauce to serve with grilled scallops or lightly poached oysters. It is extremely light, almost like a bouillon, and should be eaten with a spoon.*

**Ingredients:**

*400 g very green watercress*
*100 g butter*
*500 ml Vegetable Stock (page 10)*
*15 g soft green peppercorns*
*Salt and freshly ground pepper*

Serves 8

Preparation time: **about 25 minutes**

Cooking time: **about 25 minutes**

Cut off and discard most of the watercress stalks. In a saucepan, melt 30 g of the butter. Add the watercress and sweat it over low heat for 3 minutes, stirring continuously with a spatula.

Add the vegetable stock and green peppercorns, increase the heat to high and cook for 10 minutes. Turn off the heat and leave the sauce to infuse for 10 minutes, then pour it into a food processor and whizz for 2 minutes. Pass the sauce through a fine-mesh conical sieve into a clean saucepan, rubbing it through with the back of a ladle. Reheat until bubbling, then take the pan off the heat and whisk in the remaining butter, a little at a time. Season with salt and pepper.

# Thermidor Sauce

*This famous companion to lobster thermidor is sadly often poorly made and therefore disappointing. I enjoy it with almost all crustaceans, especially mixed with crabmeat and served au gratin. If you wish, add a teaspoon of cognac to the sauce at the end of cooking.*

**Ingredients:**

40 g shallots, very finely chopped
200 ml Fish Stock (page 13)
200 ml dry white wine
300 ml Béchamel Sauce (page 58)
100 ml double cream
1 tsp strong Dijon mustard
1 tsp English mustard powder, dissolved in a few drops of water
50 g butter, well chilled and diced
1 tbsp finely snipped tarragon
Salt and cayenne pepper

Serves 6
Preparation time: **10 minutes**
Cooking time: **about 40 minutes**

Combine the shallots, fish stock and wine in a saucepan and reduce the liquid by two-thirds. Add the béchamel and cook the sauce over low heat for 20 minutes, stirring every 5 minutes. Pour in the cream, bubble for 5 minutes, then add both mustards and cook for another 2 minutes. Turn off the heat and whisk the butter into the sauce, one piece at a time. Season with salt and a good pinch of cayenne. Finally add the tarragon and serve immediately.

# Curried Mussel Sauce

*This sauce accompanies to perfection mussels cooked à la marinière and taken out of their shells, or poached cod or halibut. It is also wonderful with a rice pilaff or a dish of pasta bows.*

Serves 6
Preparation time: **5 minutes**
Cooking time: **about 25 minutes**

**Ingredients:**
50 g butter
60 g onion, finely chopped
15 g flour
2 tsp curry powder
500 ml cooking juices from mussels and other shellfish, such as clams
1 small bouquet garni (page 9)
150 ml double cream
Salt and freshly ground pepper

Melt the butter in a saucepan, add the onion and sweat over low heat for 3 minutes. Add the curry powder (1) and flour (2), stir with a wooden spoon and cook for another 3 minutes, then pour in the cold shellfish juices. Put in the bouquet garni, bring to the boil and leave the sauce to bubble very gently for 20 minutes, stirring with the wooden spoon every 5 minutes. Add the cream (3), give another bubble, then discard the bouquet garni and season the sauce with salt and pepper. Serve immediately.

*Curried Mussel Sauce can be made with the juices from other shellfish, such as clams*

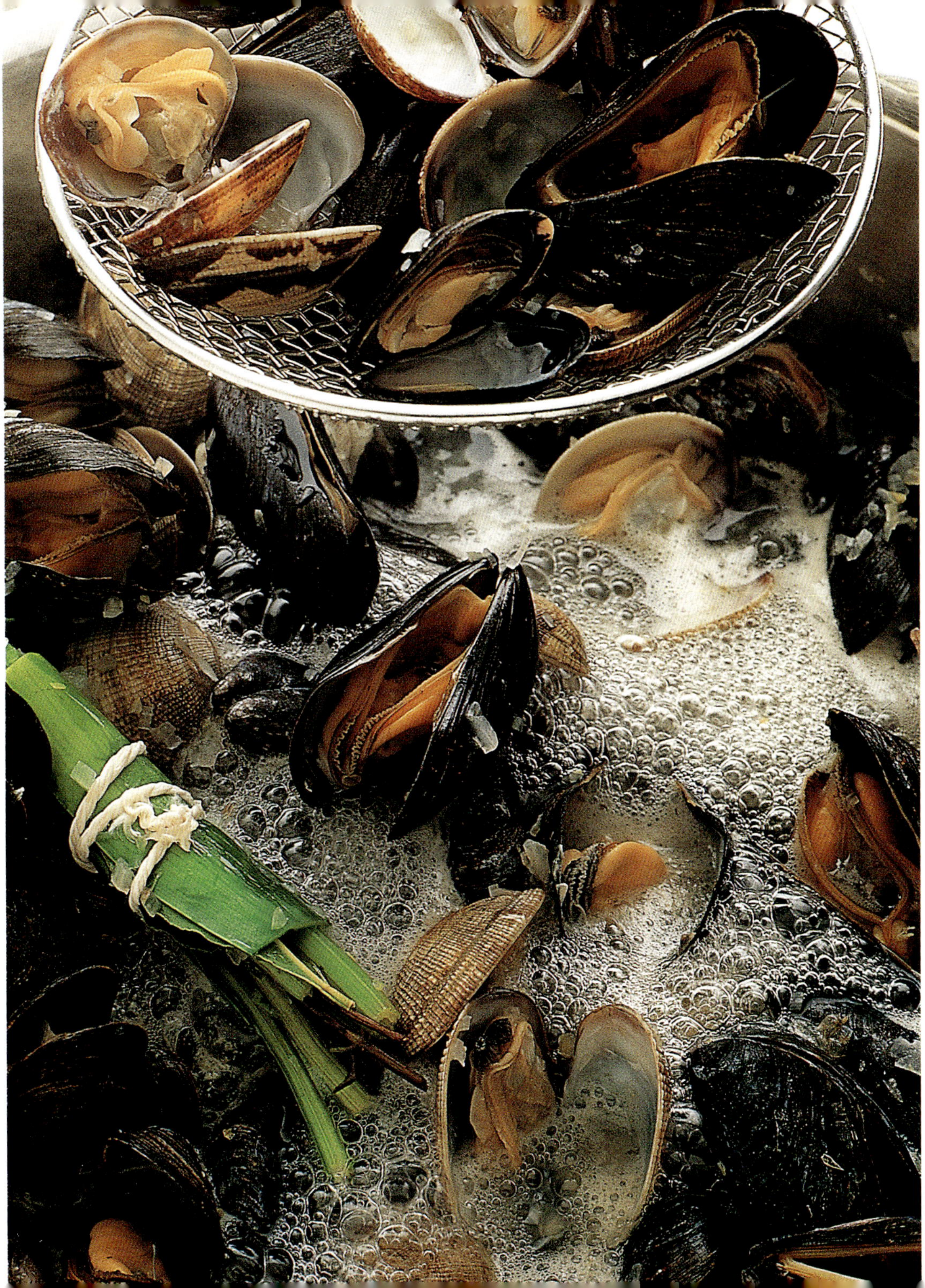

# Shrimp Sauce

*This is delicious with almost all poached, steamed or braised fish. I also love it poured over quartered hard-boiled eggs. I sometimes add a couple of tablespoons of dry sherry to the sauce just before serving.*

**Ingredients:**
600 ml Fish Stock, cooled (page 13)
40 g Blond Roux, hot (page 14)
200 ml double cream
60 g Shrimp Butter (page 23)
60 g cooked and peeled pink or brown shrimp tails
A pinch of cayenne pepper
Salt and freshly ground pepper

Serves 6
Preparation time: **15 minutes**
Cooking time: **about 45 minutes**

Put the hot roux in a saucepan, set over medium heat and whisk in the cold fish stock. As soon as it comes to the boil, reduce the heat to very low and cook gently for 30 minutes, whisking every 10 minutes and making sure that the whisk goes right into the bottom of the pan. Use a spoon to remove any skin which forms on this velouté as it cooks.

After 30 minutes, add the cream and bubble the sauce for another 10 minutes. Reduce the heat to the lowest possible (use a heat diffuser if you have one) and whisk in the shrimp butter, a little at a time. Season the sauce with salt and pepper and spice it up with cayenne to taste. Pass it through a wire-mesh conical sieve, then add the shrimp tails and serve immediately.

# Mango Sauce

This refreshing, fruity sauce is perfect for outdoor eating in summer. It is excellent with grilled or barbecued fish or with crustaceans such as lobster or langoustines.

**Ingredients:**

1 mango, about 250 g
50 ml cognac or armagnac
A small pinch of curry powder
7 g soft green peppercorns, well drained
300 ml Fish Stock (page 13)
200 ml double cream
100 g plain yoghurt
1 tbsp snipped flat-leaf parsley
Salt and freshly ground pepper

Serves 6
Preparation time: **10 minutes**
Cooking time: **about 40 minutes**

Using a knife with a fine blade, peel the mango and cut away the flesh from around the stone. Put the flesh in a saucepan with the Cognac or Armagnac, curry and green peppercorns and simmer over low heat for 5 minutes. Pour in the fish stock and bubble gently for 20 minutes. Add the cream and cook for another 5 minutes, then turn off the heat and add the yoghurt. Transfer the sauce to a blender and whizz for 30 seconds, then pass it through a wire-mesh conical sieve and season to taste with salt and pepper. Serve the sauce immediately, or keep it warm (but not too hot) in a bain-marie. Stir in the parsley just before serving.

# Sauternes Sauce with Pistachios

*I like to serve this sauce with poached or steamed fillets of sole, salmon, sea bass, turbot or John Dory. Depending on the fish, I sometimes add some freshly skinned and chopped pistachios to the sauce just before serving.*

**Ingredients:**

*20 g butter*
*150 g button mushrooms, thinly sliced*
*300 ml sweet white wine (sauternes or barsac)*
*600 ml Fish Stock (page 13)*
*75 g Blond Roux (page 14), cooled*
*80 g Pistachio Butter (page 25)*
*150 ml double cream*
*Salt and freshly ground pepper*

Serves 6
Preparation time: **10 minutes**
Cooking time: **about 40 minutes**

Melt the butter in a saucepan, add the mushrooms and sweat gently for 2 minutes. Pour in the wine, reduce by one-third, then add the stock and bring to the boil. Immediately whisk in the cooled roux, a little at a time (1). Cook the sauce at a very gentle bubble for 30 minutes, whisking and skimming the surface every 10 minutes. Add the cream and cook until the sauce coats the back of a spoon, then whisk in the pistachio butter, a small piece at a time (2). As soon as it is all incorporated, stop the cooking, season the sauce and pass it through a fine conical sieve. Serve at once, or keep it warm in a bain-marie, but do not allow it to boil.

# Matelote Sauce

*Matelote sauce goes well with pan-fried trout, whiting, monkfish and many other fish. For a red matelote use fish stock made with red wine and substitute veal stock for the fish velouté to give the sauce a deep amber colour.*

**Ingredients:**

*250 ml Fish Stock (page 13)*
*50 g button mushrooms, thinly sliced*
*400 ml Fish Velouté (page 13)*
*50 g butter, or 100 g Langoustine Butter (page 24), chilled and diced*
*Salt and cayenne pepper*

Serves 4
Preparation time: **5 minutes**
Cooking time: **about 20 minutes**

Put the fish stock and mushrooms in a saucepan and cook over medium heat until half the liquid has evaporated. Add the fish velouté and bubble the sauce gently for 10 minutes, then pass it through a wire-mesh conical sieve into a clean pan. Off the heat, whisk in the butter, a little at a time. Season the sauce to taste with salt and cayenne pepper.

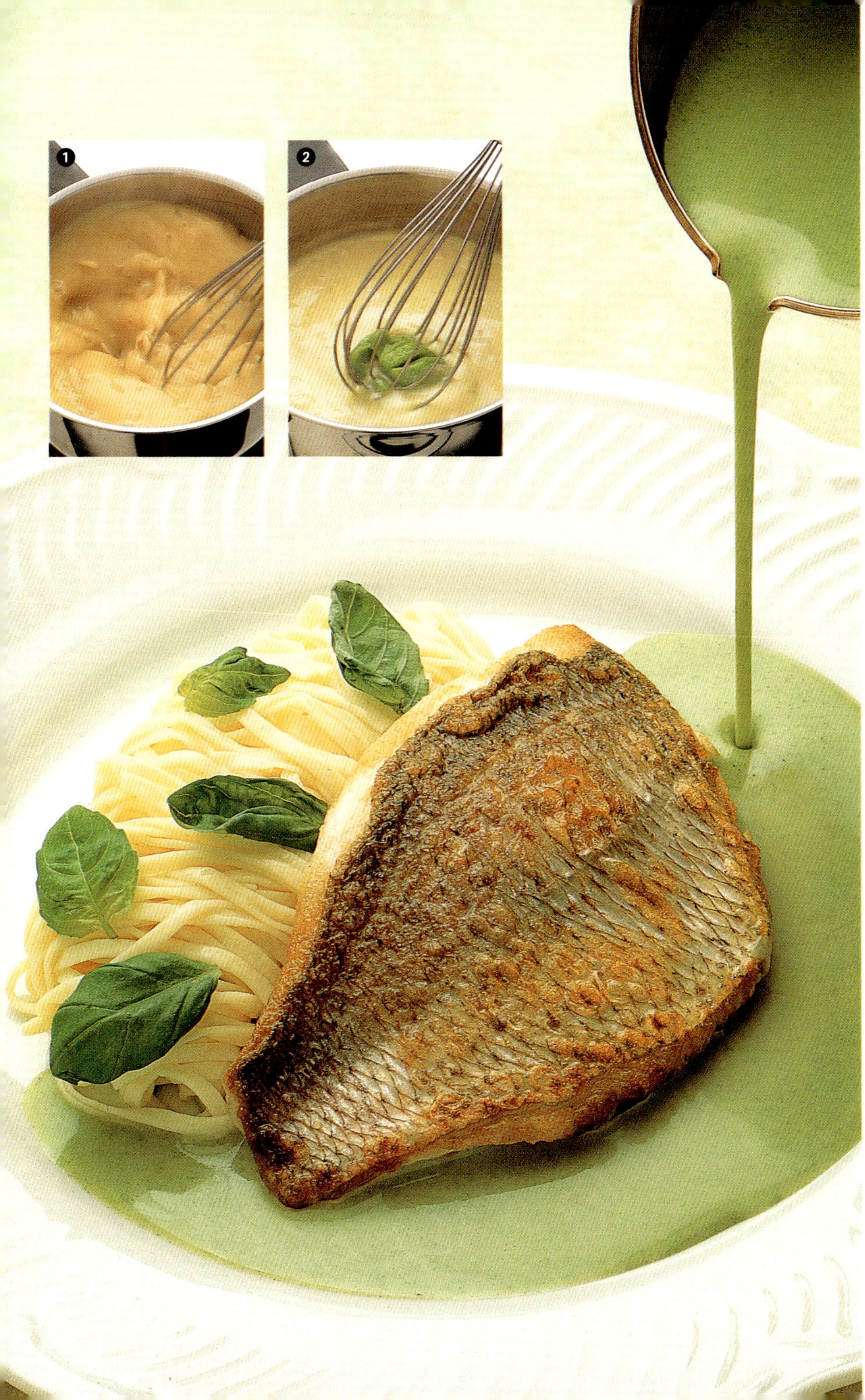
1
2

# Seaspray Sauce

*This sauce has the tang of the sea. It is excellent served with braised fish, such as turbot or halibut, or with a fish pie.*

**Ingredients:**

20 g butter
40 g shallots, chopped
200 ml Fish Stock (page 13)
150 ml dry white wine
20 g mixed dried aromatics, ground or pulverized, consisting of equal quantities of: lavender flowers, dill seeds, lime flowers, juniper berries, coriander seeds, red pimento, lemon grass
6 sheets of dried edible seaweed
200 ml double cream
6 medium oysters, shelled, with their juices
Salt and freshly ground pepper

Serves 6
Preparation time: **5 minutes**
Cooking time: **about 25 minutes**

In a saucepan, melt the butter, add the shallots and sweat them gently for 1 minute. Pour in the fish stock and wine, then add the mixed aromatics and seaweed and cook over medium heat until the liquid has reduced by half. Add the cream together with the oysters and their juices and bubble the sauce for 5 minutes.

Transfer the contents of the saucepan to a blender and whizz for 1 minute. Pass the sauce through a wire-mesh conical sieve into a small saucepan and stand it in a bain-marie. Season to taste with salt and pepper and serve immediately, or keep the sauce warm in the bain-marie for a few minutes.

# Raspberry-scented Oyster Sauce

*A sauce which subtly combines the flavours of raspberries and oysters. I poach raw oysters for just 30 seconds and serve them barely warm in a little dish with this sauce and a scattering of blanched beansprouts... Quite simply sublime!*

**Ingredients:**

30 g shallots, chopped
18 very ripe raspberries
20 g caster sugar
50 ml raspberry vinegar
8 medium oysters, shelled, with their juices
200 ml double cream
Salt and freshly ground pepper

Serves 6
Preparation time: **5 minutes**
Cooking time: **about 12 minutes**

Combine the shallots, raspberries and sugar in a small saucepan. Cook gently for 3 – 4 minutes, stirring with a wooden spoon, until you have an almost jam-like purée. Add the vinegar, bubble for 3 minutes, then add the oysters and cream and simmer gently for 5 minutes. Pour the sauce into a blender and purée for 30 seconds, then pass it through a wire-mesh conical sieve into a clean saucepan. Season to taste and serve the sauce immediately, or keep it warm for a few minutes.

# Normandy Sauce

*This classic sauce is wonderful not only with sole à la normande, but with any white fish. The addition of mussel juices makes it even more delicious.*

**Ingredients:**

30 g butter
100 g button mushrooms, thinly sliced
1 sprig of thyme
60 g White Roux, hot (page 14)
500 ml Fish Stock, cooled (page 13)
50 ml mussel juices (optional)
200 ml double cream, mixed with 3 egg yolks
Juice of $1/2$ lemon
Salt and freshly ground white pepper

Serves 6
Preparation time: **15 minutes**
Cooking time: **about 35 minutes**

In a saucepan, melt the butter over low heat, add the mushrooms and thyme and sweat them for 2 minutes. Stir in the hot white roux, then pour in the cold fish stock and mussel juices, if you are using them. Mix with a small whisk and bring to the boil. Bubble the sauce gently for 20 minutes, stirring it with the whisk every 5 minutes. Add the cream and egg yolk mixture and the lemon juice and continue to bubble the sauce gently for another 10 minutes. Season to taste with salt and white pepper, pass the sauce through a wire-mesh conical sieve and serve immediately.

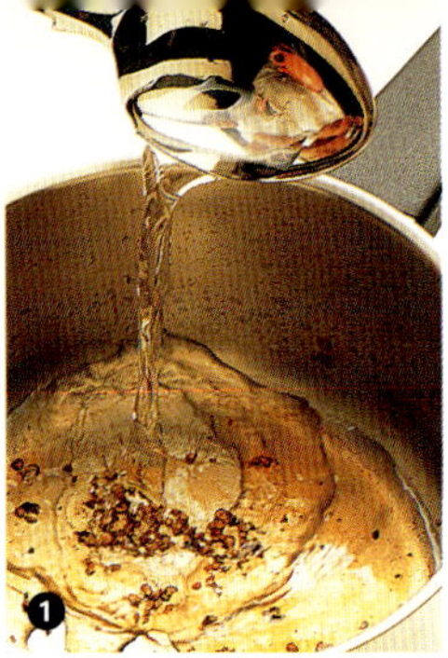

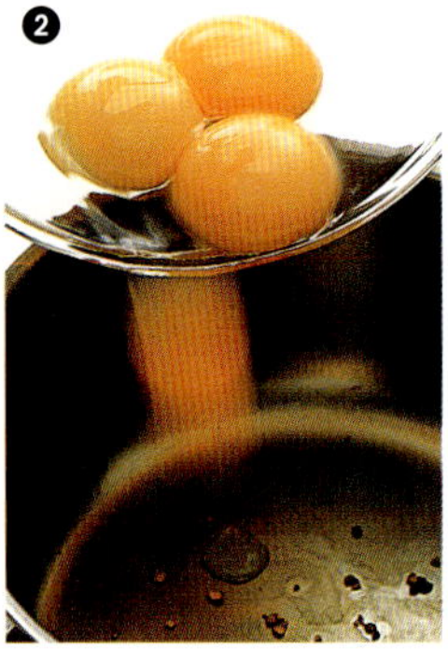

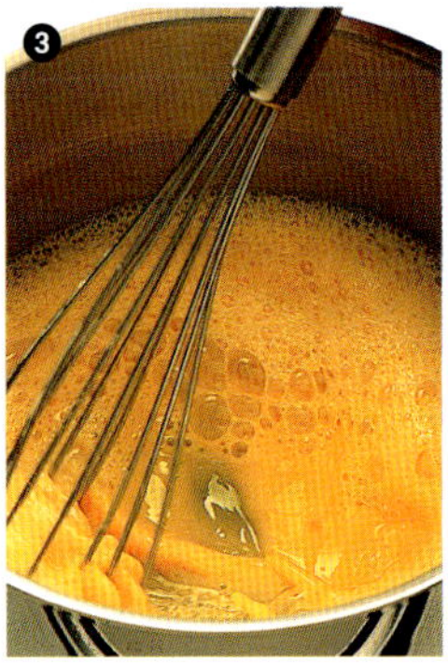

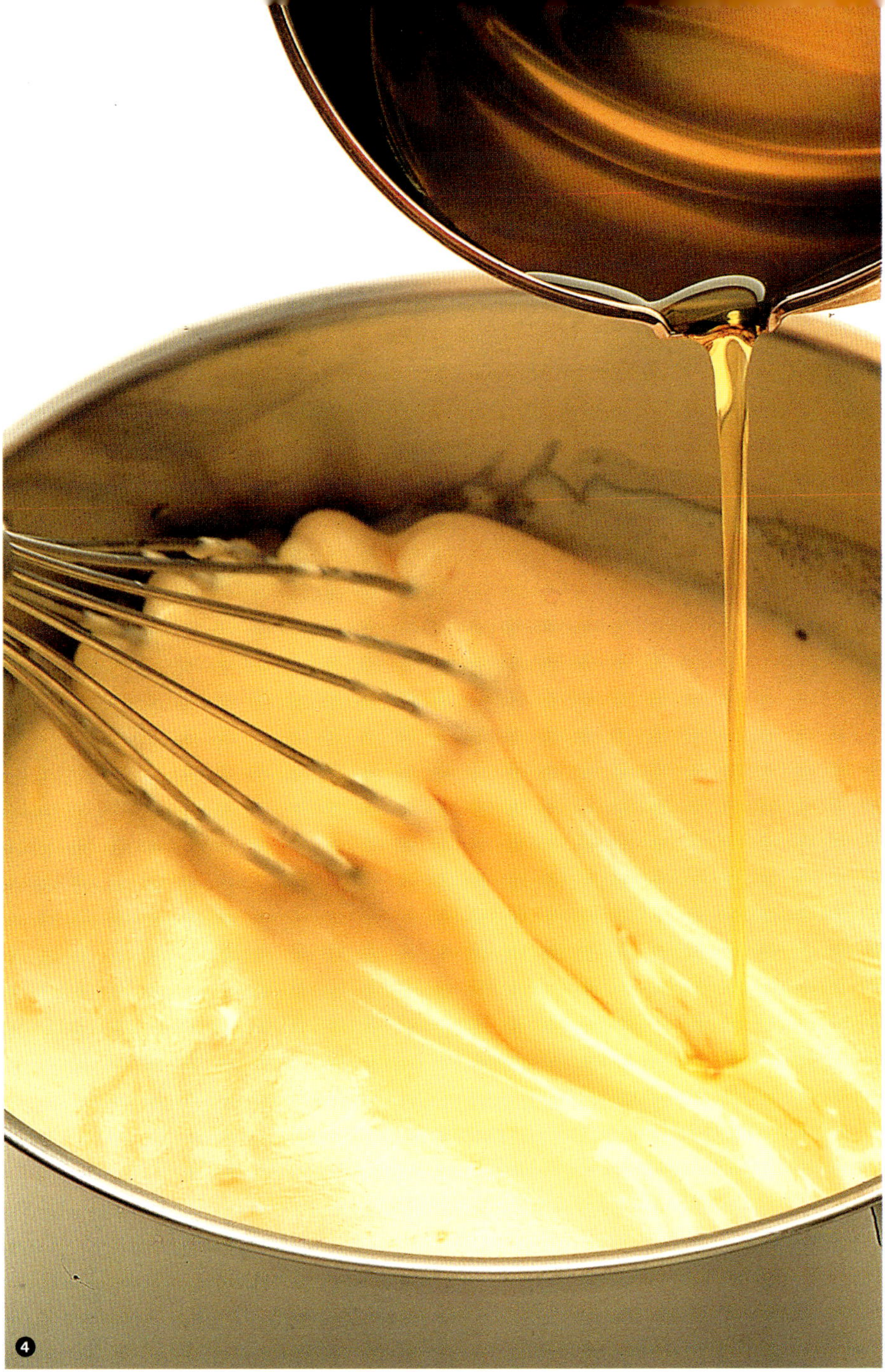

# Hollandaise Sauce

*Hollandaise Sauce is one of the great classics and many other sauces derive from it. It is light, smooth and delicate and does not like to be kept waiting; if you cannot serve it immediately, keep it covered in a warm place.*

**Ingredients:**
4 tbsp cold water
1 tbsp white wine vinegar
1 tsp white peppercorns, crushed
4 egg yolks
250 g butter, freshly clarified (page 8) and cooled to tepid
Juice of ½ lemon
Salt

Serves 6 (makes about 700 ml)
Preparation time: *20 minutes*
Cooking time: *12 – 15 minutes*

Combine the water, vinegar and pepper in a small, heavy-based stainless steel saucepan (1). Over low heat, reduce by one-third, then leave to cool in a cold place.

When the liquid is cold, add the egg yolks (2) and mix thoroughly with a small whisk. Set the saucepan over a very gentle heat and whisk continuously, making sure that the whisk comes into contact with the entire bottom surface of the pan (3). Keep whisking as you gently and progressively increase the heat source; the sauce should emulsify very gradually, becoming smooth and creamy after 8 – 10 minutes. Do not allow the temperature of the sauce to rise above 65°C.

Take the saucepan off the heat and, whisking continuously, blend in the cooled clarified butter, a little at a time (4). Season the sauce with salt to taste.

Pass the sauce through a fine-mesh conical sieve and serve as soon as possible, stirring in the lemon juice at the last moment (5).

**Noisette Sauce:** 50 g beurre noisette (browned butter) added just before serving gives hollandaise sauce a delicious flavour and transforms it into a noisette sauce. To make the browned butter heat some butter in a small saucepan until sizzling and nutty brown. Do not let it blacken and burn.

# Hollandaise Sauce with Red Butter

*I like to serve this glorious sauce with grilled lobster or a piece of pan-fried cod garnished with langoustine tails and braised oyster mushrooms.*

**Ingredients:**
1 quantity Hollandaise Sauce (page 49), made with only 150 g clarified butter
200 g Langoustine Butter (page 24)
5 g fresh ginger, finely grated
50 ml whipping cream, whipped to a floppy consistency with the juice of ½ lemon
Salt and freshly ground white pepper

Serves 6
Preparation time: **5 minutes**
Cooking time: **12 – 15 minutes**

Follow the recipe for hollandaise sauce, gradually whisking in the 150 g clarified butter and the shrimp or langoustine butter. Add the lemon juice specified in the recipe and the ginger. Very gently fold in the lemony cream, season with salt and pepper and serve immediately.

# Hollandaise Sauce with Fish Stock

*This sauce is delicious with pan-fried or grilled turbot or halibut. I sometimes add a few spoons of the cooking juices from shellfish to the fish stock before reducing it, which further enhances the sauce.*

**Ingredients:**
100 ml Fish Stock (page 13)
1 quantity Hollandaise Sauce (page 49)
1 tbsp snipped dill
50 g whipping cream, whipped to soft peaks
Salt and freshly ground white pepper

Serves 6
Preparation time: **5 minutes**
Cooking time: **about 20 minutes**

Pour the fish stock into a small saucepan and reduce over low heat to only 2 tablespoons. Whisk this reduction into the hollandaise sauce, then add the lemon juice specified in the recipe, the dill and the cream. Season to taste and serve at once.

# Mousseline Sauce

*This delicate sauce is perfect for serving with poached or steamed fish or with asparagus. When truffles are in season, I add some chopped truffle trimmings, which make the sauce even more delectable.*

**Ingredients:**
1 quantity Hollandaise Sauce (page 49)
75 ml whipping cream, whipped to soft peaks
Salt and freshly ground white pepper

*Serves 8*
*Preparation time: 5 minutes*
*Cooking time: 12 – 15 minutes*

Just before serving the sauce, whisk the lemon juice specified in the recipe and the whipped cream into the hollandaise. Season and serve immediately.

# Maltaise Sauce

*I like to serve this with crisply cooked mange-tout mixed with some orange segments and asparagus. It also goes very well with poached salmon trout.*

**Ingredients:**
Juice of 1 large blood orange (preferably), or of 2 small oranges
Zest from the orange, very finely chopped, blanched, refreshed and well drained
1 quantity Hollandaise Sauce (page 49)
Salt and freshly ground white pepper

*Serves 6*
*Preparation time: 5 minutes*
*Cooking time: 12 – 15 minutes*

Put the orange juice in a small saucepan, set over low heat and reduce by one-third, then add the zests and take the pan off the heat. Just before serving, whisk the lemon juice specified in the recipe into the hollandaise sauce, together with the reduced orange juice and zests. Serve immediately.

# Beer Sauce

*This sauce is excellent with braised fish steaks, like turbot or huss. The addition of a spoonful of the braising liquid just before serving will enhance the flavour of the sauce.*

Serves 4
Preparation time: **5 minutes**
Cooking time: **about 15 minutes**

### Ingredients:

*60 g shallots, very finely sliced*
*1 small bouquet garni (page 9)*
*4 juniper berries, crushed*
*300 ml mild light beer*
*200 ml double cream*
*60 g butter, chilled and diced*
*1/2 tbsp finely snipped flat-leaf parsley*
*Salt and freshly ground pepper*

Put the shallots, bouquet garni and juniper berries in a saucepan, pour in the beer (1) and reduce by two-thirds over medium heat (2). Add the cream (3) and bubble for 5 minutes, until the sauce will lightly coat the back of a spoon (4). If it seems too thin, cook it for a few more minutes. Pass the sauce through a conical sieve, whisk in the butter, a small piece at a time (5), and finally swirl the parsley into the sauce (6). Season to taste with salt and pepper.

# Beurre Blanc with Cream

*Like all beurres blancs, this must be made with a really good quality dry white wine and the best quality unsalted butter. This delicate sauce is simple to make and is delicious with any poached fish. For braised fish replace the wine with dry sherry.*

**Ingredients:**
100 ml white wine vinegar
60 g shallots, finely chopped
2 tbsp water
50 ml double cream
200 g butter, chilled and diced
Salt and freshly ground white pepper

Serves 6
Preparation time: **10 minutes**
Cooking time: **about 15 minutes**

Combine the vinegar, shallots and water in a small, thick-bottomed saucepan and reduce the liquid over low heat by two-thirds. Add the cream and reduce again by one-third. Over low heat, whisk in the butter, a little at a time, or beat it in with a wooden spoon. It is vital to keep the sauce barely simmering at 90°C and not to let it boil during this operation. Season with salt and pepper and serve immediately.

**Beurre Rouge with Cream:** You can make an unusual red version of this beurre blanc by substituting an equal quantity of red wine vinegar for the white wine vinegar.

# Champagne Beurre Blanc

*This sauce is wonderful with whole braised fish, such as John Dory or baby turbot.*

**Ingredients:**
50 ml champagne vinegar
60 g shallots, finely chopped
1 sprig of thyme
100 ml brut champagne
60 g button mushrooms, very finely diced
250 g butter, chilled and diced
Salt and freshly ground white pepper

Serves 6
Preparation time: **10 minutes**
Cooking time: **about 20 minutes**

Combine the vinegar, shallots and thyme in a small, thick-bottomed saucepan and reduce the liquid by half over low heat. Add the champagne and mushrooms and continue to cook gently until the liquid has again reduced by half. Remove the thyme. Over low heat, whisk in the butter, a little at a time, or beat it in with a wooden spoon. It is vital to keep the sauce barely simmering at 90°C and not to let it boil during this operation. Season to taste and serve the sauce at once, or keep it hot in a bain-marie for a few minutes.

# Cider Beurre Blanc

*I adore this butter sauce served with grilled scallops, a simply poached sole on the bone, braised turbot or a John Dory roasted in the oven and served whole at the table.*

**Ingredients:**
80 ml cider vinegar
60 g shallots, finely chopped
100 ml sweet cider
50 g dessert apple (preferably Cox), peeled and finely grated
250 g butter, chilled and diced
Salt and freshly ground pepper

Serves 6
Preparation time: **10 minutes**
Cooking time: **15 minutes**

Put the vinegar and shallots in a small, thick-bottomed saucepan, set over low heat and reduce the liquid by half. Add the cider and grated apple and cook gently to reduce the liquid by one-third. Still over low heat, incorporate the butter, a little at a time, using a whisk or small wooden spoon. The butter sauce must not boil, but merely tremble at about 90°C. Season to taste with salt and pepper and serve immediately, or keep the sauce warm for a few minutes in a bain-marie.

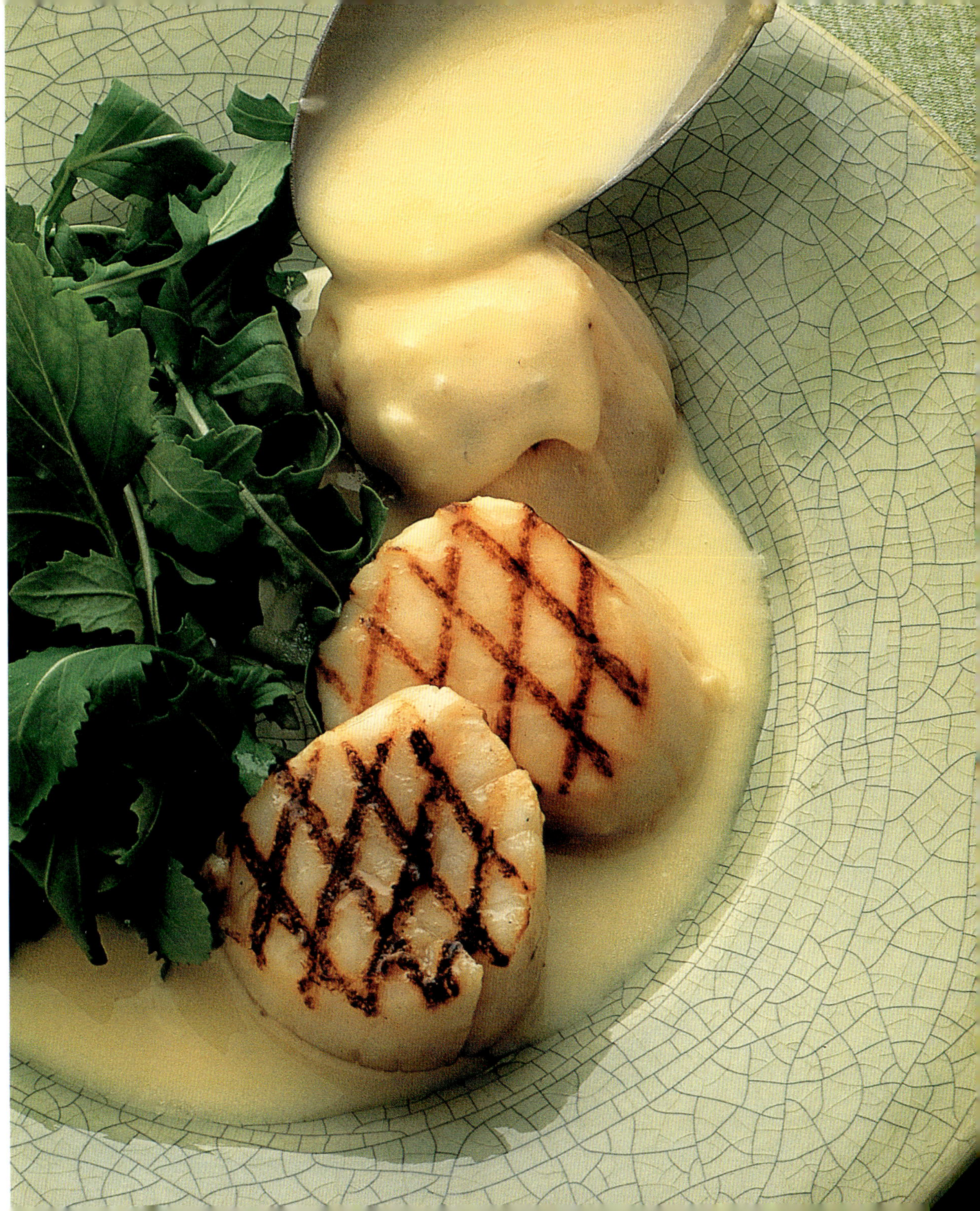

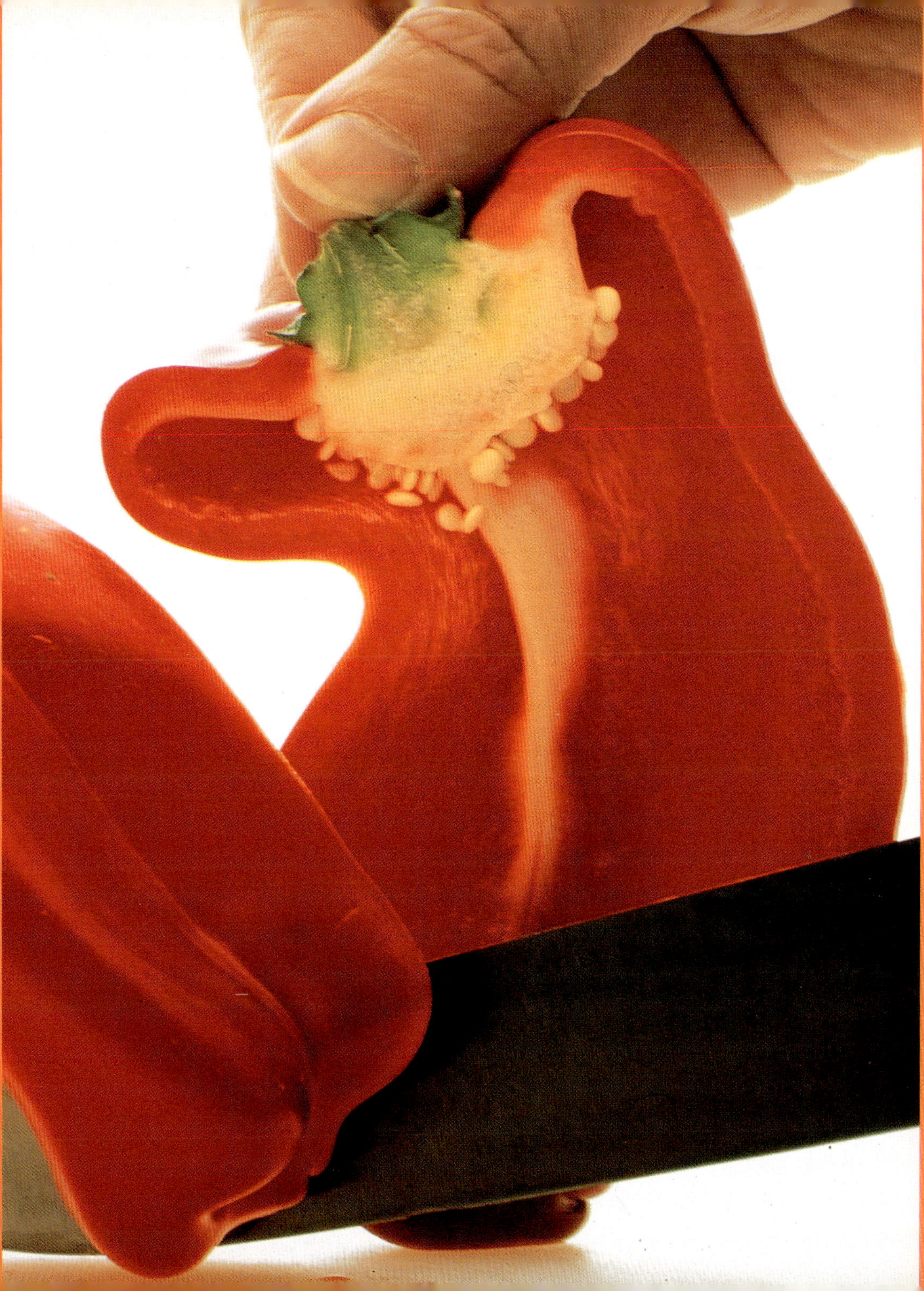

# Red Pepper Sabayon

*I serve this sabayon with poached eggs on a bed of pilaff rice, or with vegetables like cauliflower and asparagus. It is also good with grilled fish, particularly salmon escalopes. The vegetable stock can be replaced by chicken or fish stock, depending on the dish the sauce is to accompany.*

**Ingredients:**

200 g red pepper
200 ml Vegetable Stock (page 10) or Fish Stock (page 13)
1 small sprig of thyme
4 egg yolks
60 g butter, chilled and diced
Salt and freshly ground pepper

Serves 4
Preparation time: **10 minutes**
Cooking time: **about 25 minutes**

Halve the red pepper lengthways (left) and remove the stalk, seeds and white membranes. Coarsely chop the pepper, place it in a small saucepan with the stock and thyme (1) and simmer for 15 minutes. Pour the contents of the saucepan into a blender and whizz for 1 minute. Pass the purée through a wire-mesh conical sieve into a small clean saucepan and leave until almost cold, then whisk in the egg yolks (2). Stand the pan in a bain-marie or on a heat diffuser over low heat and whisk the sabayon to a ribbon consistency (3). Whisk in the butter, a little at a time (4), season the sabayon with salt and pepper and serve at once.

**Halve the red pepper lengthways**

# Béchamel Sauce

*This is the ideal sauce for any number of dishes, such as cauliflower or endive au gratin, macaroni cheese made with a touch of cream and grated gruyère or emmenthal, a genuine croque monsieur – the list is endless. Like hollandaise and mayonnaise, béchamel forms the basis of innumerable other sauces.*

**Ingredients:**
500 ml milk
60 g White Roux (page 14), cooled
Freshly grated nutmeg (optional)
Salt and freshly ground white pepper

Serves 4
Preparation time: **5 minutes**
Cooking time: **about 25 minutes**

Put the cold roux into a small, thick-bottomed saucepan. Bring the milk to the boil and pour it on to the roux, mixing and stirring with a whisk or wooden spatula. Set the pan over low heat and bring the mixture to the boil, still stirring continuously. As soon as it reaches boiling point, reduce the heat and cook at a very gentle simmer for about 20 minutes, stirring the sauce continuously (1) and making sure that the spatula or whisk scrapes across all the surfaces of the pan.

Season the sauce with salt, white pepper and a very little nutmeg if you wish (2), then pass it through a conical strainer (3). You can serve it immediately or keep it warm in a bain-marie, in which case dot a few flakes of butter over the surface to prevent a skin from forming (4).

Béchamel sauce will keep in an airtight container in the fridge for a maximum of four days.

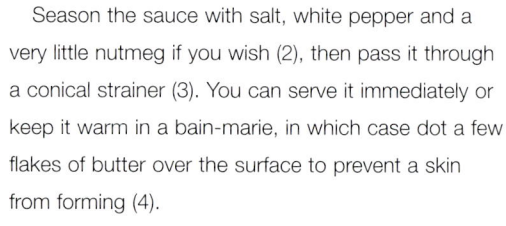

*Béchamel Sauce forms the basis of innumerable other sauces*

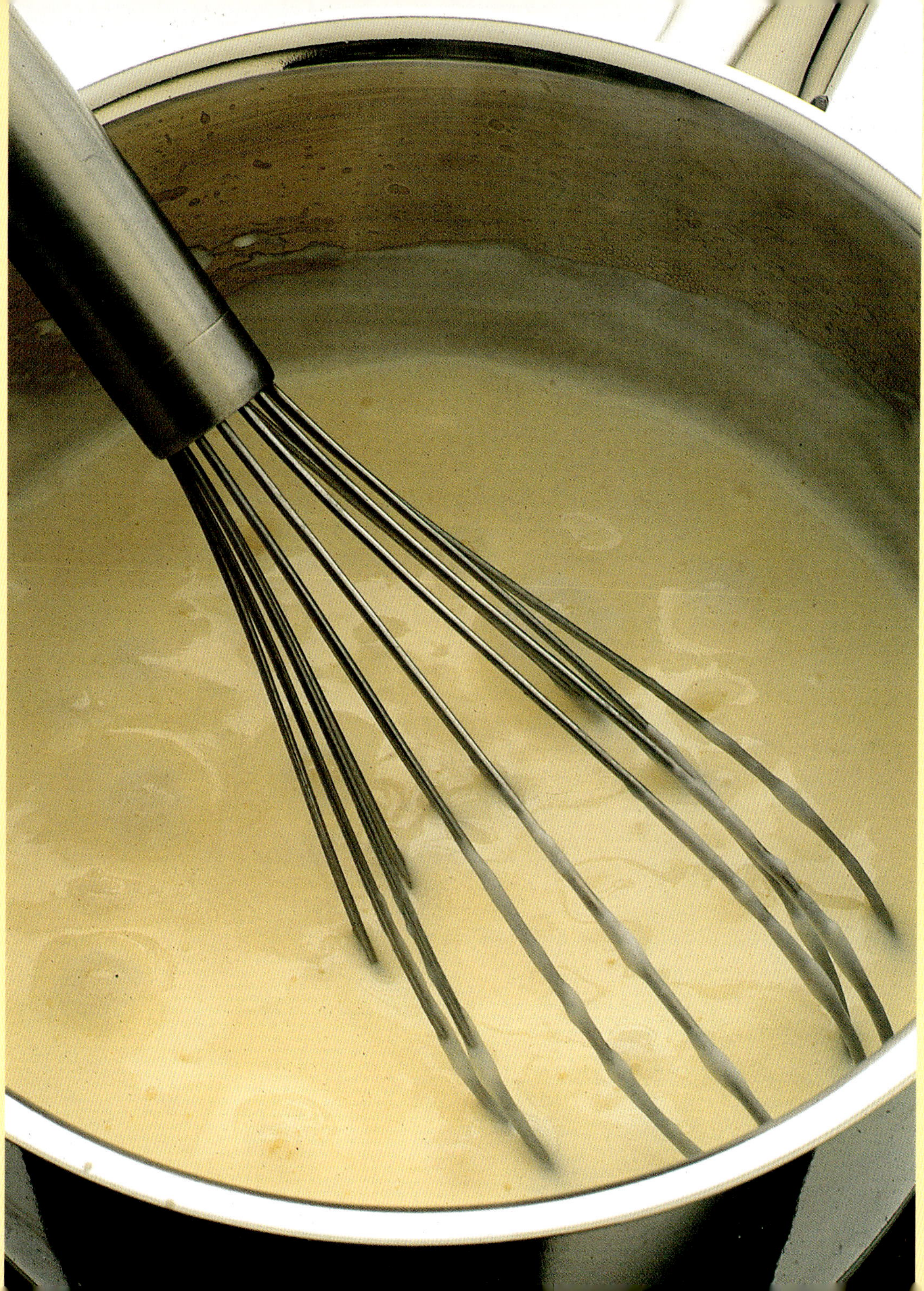

# Coconut and Chilli Pepper Sauce

*Serve this unusual spicy sauce with wide noodles or any poached firm-fleshed white fish.*

Serves 8
Preparation time: *10 minutes*
Cooking time: *25 minutes*

### Ingredients:
*100 g butter*
*10 g small hot red chillies, deseeded and finely chopped*
*20 g hot green Jalapeño peppers, deseeded and finely chopped*
*250 g small peeled shrimps or prawns (optional)*

### For the coconut béchamel:
*30 g butter*
*30 g flour*
*400 ml canned coconut milk*
*Freshly grated nutmeg*
*Salt and freshly ground pepper*
*2 garlic cloves, crushed or finely chopped*
*1 tbsp soy sauce*

First make the coconut béchamel. In a small saucepan, melt the 30 g butter and stir in the flour to make a roux. Cook over low heat for 2 minutes, stirring all the time with a whisk. Add the coconut milk, bring to the boil, then immediately season with nutmeg, salt and pepper and cook gently for 20 minutes, stirring continuously. Off the heat, stir in the soy sauce and garlic.

In another small saucepan, heat the 100 g butter until it turns fragrant and golden brown. Toss in the chopped chillies (1) and immediately tip the mixture into the coconut béchamel and stir until well amalgamated (2). Adjust the seasoning if necessary and stir in the shrimps at the last moment, if you are using them (3). Serve the sauce hot.

# Mustard and White Wine Sauce

*This versatile sauce is perfect served with any poached or braised firm-fleshed fish.*

**Ingredients:**

30 g butter
80 g button mushrooms, thinly sliced
60 g shallots, finely chopped
a pinch of curry powder
1 tbsp cognac or armagnac
200 ml dry white wine
1 small bouquet garni (page 9)
200 ml Fish Stock (page 13)
300 ml double cream
1 tsp English mustard powder, dissolved in a little water
2 tbsp wholegrain mustard
salt and freshly ground pepper

Serves 4
Preparation time: **10 minutes**
Cooking time: **about 40 minutes**

In a saucepan, melt the butter, add the mushrooms and shallots and sweat for 1 minute (1). Stir in the curry powder and add the cognac or armagnac and wine (2). Bring to the boil, put in the bouquet garni and reduce the liquid by one-third. Pour in the fish or chicken stock, bubble for 5 minutes, then add the cream and the English mustard and cook until the sauce is thick enough to coat the bowl of a spoon (3). Remove the bouquet garni, season to taste with salt and pepper and pass the sauce through a wire-mesh conical strainer. Stir in the wholegrain mustard (4). The sauce is now ready to serve.

Sauces for Fish and Shellfish

# Mornay Sauce

*You can coat a multitude of dishes with this sauce and immediately lightly brown them under a hot grill or salamander: poached fish, eggs, vegetables and white meats are all excellent served this way. Mixed with macaroni, mornay sauce also makes a delicious macaroni cheese.*

**Ingredients:**

1 quantity boiling Béchamel Sauce (page 58)
50 ml double cream mixed with 3 egg yolks
100 g emmenthal, gruyère or farmhouse cheddar, finely grated
Salt and freshly ground pepper

Serves 4
Preparation time: **5 minutes**
Cooking time: **about 2 minutes**

Add the cream and egg yolk mixture to the boiling béchamel and bubble for 1 minute, whisking vigorously. Turn off the heat and mix in your chosen cheese with a wooden spoon. Season the sauce with salt and pepper and use it as you wish.

# White Bordelaise or Bonnefoy Sauce

*This robust, well-structured sauce makes the perfect accompaniment to fish with a rather bland flavour, such as whiting, lemon sole, farmed trout or huss.*

**Ingredients:**

300 ml dry white wine
30 ml cognac
60 g shallots, finely chopped
1 bouquet garni (page 9)
400 ml Fish Velouté (page 13)
40 g butter, chilled and diced
1 tbsp snipped tarragon leaves
Salt and freshly ground pepper

Serves 4
Preparation time: **5 minutes**
Cooking time: **about 30 minutes**

Combine the wine, cognac, shallots and bouquet garni in a saucepan and reduce the liquid to one-third over high heat. Add the fish velouté and bubble the sauce gently for 20 minutes, skimming the surface whenever necessary. Pass the sauce through a wire-mesh conical sieve into a clean pan, then whisk in the butter, a little at a time. Season the sauce with salt and pepper, stir in the tarragon and serve.

# Index

**A**
Américaine sauce, 30-1
anchovy butter, 25
apples: cider beurre blanc, 54
asparagus coulis, 20
aspic, 13

**B**
basil: fish fumet with tomatoes, 33
béchamel sauce, 58-9
    mornay sauce, 62
    thermidor sauce, 39
beer sauce, 52
Bercy sauce, 32
beurre blanc:
    champagne, 54
    cider, 54-5
    with cream, 53
beurre noisette: noisette sauce, 49
beurre rouge with cream, 53
blond roux, 14
bones: fish stock or fumet, 12-13
    fishbone sauce, 19
butter, 8
    anchovy butter, 25
    beurre blanc with cream, 53
    beurre rouge with cream, 53
    champagne beurre blanc, 54
    cider beurre blanc, 54
    hollandaise sauce, 48-9
    hollandaise sauce with red butter, 50
    langoustine butter, 24
    noisette sauce, 49
    pistachio butter, 25
    shrimp butter, 22-3

**C**
carrot coulis, 20
champagne beurre blanc, 54
champagne sauce, 28
cheese, 8
    fresh goat's cheese sauce with rosemary, 19
    mornay sauce, 62
chillies: coconut and chilli pepper sauce, 60
cider beurre blanc, 54
claret sauce, 32
coconut and chilli pepper sauce, 60
cognac: Américaine sauce, 30-1
    mango sauce, 43
    white Bordelaise or Bonnefoy sauce, 62
coulis: asparagus, 20
    cooked tomato, 34-5
    leek with curry, 21
    light carrot, 20
crayfish: crustacean oil, 26-7
    langoustine butter, 24
    Nantua sauce, 29
cream, 8
    beer sauce, 52
    beurre blanc with cream, 53
    beurre rouge with cream, 53
    champagne sauce, 28
    mango sauce, 43
    mousseline sauce, 51
    mustard and white wine sauce, 61
    Normandy sauce, 47
    raspberry-scented oyster sauce, 47
    seafood sauce with saffron, 28
    seaspray sauce, 46
    shrimp sauce, 42
    thermidor sauce, 39
crème fraîche, 8
crustacean oil, 26-7
curry powder, 9
    curried mussel sauce, 40-1
    fromage blanc sauce with curry, 18
    leek coulis with curry, 21
    mango sauce, 43

**D**
dairy products, 8
deglazing, 8

**E**
eggs: hollandaise sauce, 48-9

**F**
fines herbes, 9
fish fumet with tomatoes, 33
fish stock or fumet, 12-13
fish velouté, 13
    matelote sauce, 44
fishbone sauce, 19
freezing stocks, 10
fromage blanc, 8
    fromage blanc sauce with curry, 18
fumet: fish, 12-13
    fish with tomatoes, 33

**G**
gelatine: aspic, 13
goat's cheese sauce with rosemary, 19
green peppercorns: watercress sauce, 38

**H**
herbs, 9
    yoghurt sauce, 18
hollandaise sauce, 48-9
    mousseline sauce, 51
    with fish stock, 50
    with red butter, 50

**L**
langoustines: crustacean oil, 26-7
    langoustine butter, 24
    Nantua sauce, 29
leek coulis with curry, 21
lemon grass, parsley nage with, 37
light carrot coulis, 20
lobster: Américaine sauce, 30-1

**M**
Maltaise sauce, 51
mandarin sauce, 36
mango sauce, 43
matelote sauce, 44
mayonnaise, 15
    yoghurt sauce, 18
mornay sauce, 62
mousseline sauce, 51
mushrooms: champagne sauce, 28
    claret sauce, 32
    mustard and white wine sauce, 61
    Normandy sauce, 47
    sauternes sauce with pistachios, 44
    tomato nage, 33
mussels: curried mussel sauce, 40-1
    Normandy sauce, 47
mustard and white wine sauce, 61

**N**
nages: parsley with lemon grass, 37
    tomato, 33
    vegetable, 10
Nantua sauce, 29
noisette sauce, 49
Normandy sauce, 47

**O**
oil, crustacean, 26-7
orange: light carrot coulis, 20
    Maltaise sauce, 51
    mandarin sauce, 36
oysters: raspberry-scented oyster sauce, 47
    seaspray sauce, 46

**P**
parsley nage with lemon grass, 37
pepper, 9

# Index

peppers: fish fumet with tomatoes, 33
red pepper sabayon, 56-7
pistachio nuts: pistachio butter, 25
sauternes sauce with pistachios, 44

**R**
raspberry-scented oyster sauce, 47
red pepper sabayon, 56-7
rosemary, fresh goat's cheese sauce with, 19
roux: blond, 14
white, 14

**S**
sabayon, red pepper, 56-7
saffron, 9
seafood sauce with saffron, 28
salt, 9
sauternes sauce with pistachios, 44
seasonings, 9
seaspray sauce, 46
shallots, 9
Bercy sauce, 32
champagne sauce, 28
claret sauce, 32
shellfish cooking juices, 9
seafood sauce with saffron, 28
shrimp: coconut and chilli pepper sauce, 60
shrimp butter, 22-3
shrimp sauce, 42
spices, 9
stocks: cooling and freezing, 10
fish, 12-13
vegetable, 10-11
straining sauces, 8

**T**
tarragon: thermidor sauce, 39
white Bordelaise or Bonnefoy sauce, 62
thermidor sauce, 39
tomatoes: Américaine sauce, 30-1
cooked tomato coulis, 34-5
fish fumet with tomatoes, 33
Nantua sauce, 29
peeling, 34
tomato nage, 33

yoghurt sauce, 18

**V**
vegetable stock or nage, 10-11
velouté: fish, 13
matelote sauce, 44
vinegar: beurre blanc with cream, 53
champagne beurre blanc, 54

**W**
warming sauces, 8
watercress sauce, 38
white Bordelaise or Bonnefoy sauce, 62
white roux, 14
wine: Américaine sauce, 30-1
Bercy sauce, 32
champagne sauce, 28
claret sauce, 32
fishbone sauce, 19
mustard and white wine sauce, 61
sauternes sauce with pistachios, 44
seaspray sauce, 46
thermidor sauce, 39
white Bordelaise or Bonnefoy sauce, 62

**Y**
yoghurt, 8
mango sauce, 43
yoghurt sauce, 18

# Acknowledgements

This edition published in 2000 by
Quadrille Publishing Ltd
Alhambra House
27–31 Charing Cross Road
London WC2H 0LS

Based on material originally published in *Sauces; sweet and savoury, classic and new* by Michel Roux.

Text © 1996 & 2000 Michel Roux
Photography © 1996 Martin Brigdale
Design & layout © 2000 Quadrille Publishing Ltd

Publishing director: **Anne Furniss**
Art Director: **Mary Evans**
Art Editor: **Rachel Gibson**
Project editor & translator: **Kate Whiteman**
Editorial Assistant: **Caroline Perkins**
Styling: **Helen Trent**
Production: **Rachel Wells**

All rights reserved. No part of this book may be reproduced, stored in a retrieval system or transmitted in any form or by any means, electronic, electrostatic, magnetic tape, mechanical, photocopying, recording or otherwise, without the permission in writing of the publisher.

The right of Michel Roux to be identified as the Author of this Work has been asserted by him in accordance with the Copyright, Designs and Patents Act 1988.

Cataloguing-in-Publication Date: a catalogue record for this book is available from the British Library.

ISBN 1 902757 40 8

Printed & bound by Dai Nippon Printing Company Ltd, Hong Kong